GEOGRAPHY
ACROSS
THE CURRICULUM

The Authors

Dennis Reinhartz is Associate Professor of History and Russian Language at the University of Texas at Arlington. He is the coauthor of *Teach-Practice-Apply: The TPA Instruction Model, 7–12*, published by NEA.

Judy Reinhartz is Professor of Education, Center for Professional Teacher Education, at the University of Texas at Arlington. She is the coauthor of *Teach-Practice-Apply: The TPA Instruction Model, K–8*, *Teach-Practice-Apply: The TPA Instruction Model, 7–12*, and *Improving Middle School Instruction: A Research-Based Self-Assessment System*; and the editor of *Perspectives on Effective Teaching and the Cooperative Classroom*, and *Teacher Induction*, published by NEA.

The Advisory Panel

Jack Bradford, Mathematics Department, Flathead High School, Kalispell, Montana

Debbie Catley, Mathematics Resource Teacher, Myrtle Beach Elementary School, South Carolina

Ronald G. Helms, Teacher of the Gifted, Kettering City Schools, and Adjunct Associate Professor of Social Studies Methods, Wright State University, Ohio

Barbara S. LaPointe, Teacher, Waterbury Elementary School, Vermont

Jeanette Devone Meloro, Reading and Mathematics Teacher, Borough School, Morris Plains, New Jersey

Timothy L. Morris, Mathematics and Computer Science Instructor, Sherwood High School, North Dakota

Frances Miller Rash, Social Studies Teacher, Davidson County Schools, North Carolina

Elizabeth S. Walter, Elementary Teacher, Shepherdstown, West Virginia

Marjorie B. Weest, PSEA-R, Havertown, Pennsylvania

Judith Winzenz, English Teacher, Appleton, Wisconsin

GEOGRAPHY ACROSS THE CURRICULUM

Dennis Reinhartz
Judy Reinhartz

nea PROFESSIONAL LIBRARY
National Education Association
Washington, D.C.

To our mothers,
Ella Reinhartz and Filomena Gervasi.

—Dennis Reinhartz
Judy Reinhartz

Printing History
    First Printing: November 1990
    Second Printing: September 1992

Note

The opinions expressed in this publication should not be construed as representing the policy or position of the National Education Association. Materials published by the NEA Professional Library are intended to be discussion documents for teachers who are concerned with specialized interests of the profession.

Library of Congress Cataloging-in-Publication Data
Reinhartz, Dennis.
   Geography across the curriculum   Dennis Reinhartz, Judy
   Reinhartz.
      p. cm. — (Analysis and action series)
Includes bibliographical references.
ISBN 0–8106–3070–2
1. Geography—Study and teaching.   I. Reinhartz, Judy.
II. Title.   III. Series.
G73.R43   1990   90–5523
910.7103—dc20   CIP

CONTENTS

PREFACE

Many reasons can be given for the recent revival of geographic education. Foremost among them, the rapid movement among nations toward an ever-more interdependent global civilization became evident in the 1980s, despite popular ignorance of this phenomenon, especially in the highly developed countries (33).* Also, a "selective xenophobia," or a blocking out of geographic information not deemed relevant to a particular local or national experience, was not uncommon. For example, the United States was caught off guard by the Soviet invasion of Afghanistan in 1979 in part because few Americans knew much about Afghanistan and still fewer knew enough to care. These factors have resulted in a renewed interest in geography and a subsequent rejuvenation of geographic education. Nowhere has this progress been greater than in the United States. It is to this revitalization, and, through it, to an increase in global understanding among students and teachers, that this monograph seeks to make a contribution.

Our purpose is not to argue for the importance or disciplinary integrity of geography, or for its place in the school curriculum; we accept these as a given and endorse the urgency of teaching geography at all grade levels. Nor do we offer suggestions on how to teach geography as such. Instead, we confine our efforts to presenting ways in which the teaching of geography can be integrated into other areas of the curriculum, such as history and social studies, the humanities, science, and mathematics. It is our hope that these suggestions will help teachers expand their geographic educational skills and thereby enhance their students' learning and knowledge.

We suggest that school systems consider using an integrative approach to teaching geography. This is not to imply that if geography already exists as a separate subject it be dropped. We recommend that if geography is taught at only one or possibly two levels, the use of an integrative approach at other levels would acquaint students with geography at several other points in their education while taking social studies, humanities, and science classes. Thus, we approach the integration process from a geographic vantage point.

---

*Numbers in parentheses appearing in the text refer to the Bibliography beginning on page 87.

9

The integration of geography provides students with many opportunities to use information, skills, and concepts in a specific subject and to relate that subject to geography or vice versa. Since we are promoting geographic literacy through the study of other subjects, seeing the larger picture may help students recognize the unity of all knowledge and may in the long run be the greater contribution of this monograph.

The integration of geography into other subjects encourages students to organize their ideas into units that tend to fit into the whole fabric of knowledge; it also discourages fragmentation. As Lemlech points out, "ideas are broadly related across subject fields" (30, p. 88). Geography can enhance the teaching of science, for example, when studying about colors that absorb heat. The discussion can focus on clothing worn around the world and the location of countries whose inhabitants wear light-colored clothing and whose daily temperatures hover in the upper 90 F. range. Is there a relationship between the color of clothes people wear, the location of the country in which they live, and its distance from the sun? In the end, we hope all subject areas are enhanced by emphasizing a geographic dimension.

Although we endorse the integration of geographic education into nongeographic areas, our conception of geography, as delineated in Chapter 2, like that of Halford Mackinder, is essentially of a unified whole (11) rather than an approach through its various social, cultural, historical, and other subdivisions. And while the ideas we advance generally are applicable to grades K–12, our emphasis is on grades 4–12.

Our purpose, then, is to begin to fill a void by integrating or, more accurately, infusing geography into the school curriculum. Teachers at various grade levels and in numerous subject areas can help to eradicate geographic illiteracy and greatly broaden the global dimensions of American education. The world is no longer a we-they, American-non-American situation; we are continuing to become more interdependent on each other than ever before in history. "Without geographically literate citizens, America cannot compete in global markets or take the lead in meeting international, political, economic, environmental, social, and military challenges" (18, p. 15). We hope that this text will help to build a broad base of support for teaching and studying geography by integrating it across the curriculum. "Our future is not a gift we can take for granted; it is an achievement that must be earned" (18, p. 15).

PART I. INTRODUCTION

Chapter 1

GEOGRAPHIC EDUCATION IN THE UNITED STATES: THE CURRENT STATUS

THE PROBLEM OF GEOGRAPHIC ILLITERACY

For over a decade, numerous studies, reports, and polls have pointed out the problem of American geographic illiteracy and its consequences for the United States in a global age (50). The real problem is not only that Americans are ignorant of geography generally, but that they do not yet see the need to be well informed about the world around them. They view geography as an esoteric and/or archaic discipline, neither comprehending the value of such knowledge nor realizing that some understanding of it is essential to becoming a well-rounded, educated person. As Gilbert M. Grosvenor has pointed out, the consequences of this problem can be disastrous:

Can you imagine a banker making sage decisions about international loans with no geographic knowledge of the countries involved? Or a statesman considering the international ramifications of acid rain with no understanding of wind patterns? Or a physician treating tropical diseases with no comprehension of the complex tropical environments in which those diseases thrive?

Without a fundamental background in geography, it is not possible to fully comprehend these issues, much less find the appropriate solutions to the problems with which they are associated.

Geographic ignorance has become so critical in the United States that we are flirting with danger. Knowledge of geography is not just a nice idea; it is essential to our well-being as individuals and to our national strength and survival as a world leader . . . .

Not one of us in this country should rest until the level of geographic literacy is raised to such proportions that our children will be able to function as thoughtful, intelligent citizens of this nation and of this world. (21, p. 2)

The reasons for American geographic illiteracy are diverse and complex. Certainly, the problem reflects the decline of geographic education in elementary and secondary schools over the past quarter century. It also reflects the turmoil in the geography profession and in the teaching of geography in American higher education during the same period of time.

But American geographic ignorance is also a product of American geography. Prior to World War I, the nation developed in a unique environment for over three centuries in a hemisphere away from the rest of the world. In this relative isolation it developed its own political, economic, and social forms and attitudes. Rising rapidly to greatness, it appeared on the world scene somewhat reluctantly in the post-Civil War era. This tradition of isolation combined with an almost meteoric ascension to great power status has led to a certain egotism of insularity in American society. Partly as a result of the growth, spread, and legacy of the British Empire and partly as a result of American dominance, the global language has become English, the new Latin of the modern world, especially in the dynamic spheres of science, technology, and international business, thereby further reinforcing American insularity. In short, the United States has become used to running the world, but at a distance.

Today, American global leadership is no longer so simple or absolute. And the distance between nations no longer exists. The world and the United States with it are making a dynamic transition to a global civilization. A continuing leadership role will depend on a growing American comprehension of the world and the global processes leading into the future.

Economically, politically, or intellectually, we can no longer afford to remain geographically illiterate. Like literacy in language, geographical literacy "depends upon and contributes to the improvement of any population's cultural literacy" (36, p. 2). Unless Americans sharpen their understanding of their own geography, they will have difficulty understanding the rest of the world" (36, p. 3).

The geographical illiteracy of students reflects the archaic American attitude that "the world needs me, so let it come to me." To meet the challenges of the future, American students must be educated to help them break out of their insularity to become aware of a world beyond their county line and to understand the world and the complex interdependence of nations. Ignorance of other lands and peoples, of their customs and languages, is no longer tolerable if future generations are to play effective leadership roles internationally and if they are to continue to enjoy the best of what the world has to offer.

INTEGRATING GEOGRAPHY ACROSS THE CURRICULUM

This monograph suggests that geography be infused into the existing school curriculum rather than adding it as another separate subject at various levels. Goodlad (20) supports such an approach, cautioning that "given the present state of clutter in the curriculum . . . it is better to encourage teachers . . . to orient their current courses so as to reflect a global perspective" (p. 486). Backler (4), Kirman (28), Grosvenor (23), and Muir and Cheek (35) agree.

Our approach suggests ways to integrate relevant geographic knowledge, concepts, and skills into specific elementary and secondary subjects. (See Figure 1.1 and Part II for specific examples.) When using an integrative approach, all teachers expand their instruction to include geographic content, thus helping to promote geographic literacy skills. For us, the goal of geographic education

is to teach knowledge about the earth, to use that knowledge for personal enlightenment and development, and to apply it in making important personal decisions and in participating intelligently in societal decision making that affects our lives. (36, p. 1)

We recognize that integrating geography into existing subjects in the K–12 curriculum will not automatically solve the problem of geographic illiteracy. We offer this text as one possible solution for dealing with the problem. As the Joint Committee on Geographic Education expressed it,

Geographic education alone cannot remedy [all the] deficiencies nor can it resolve important international problems. However, training in geography gives us unique perspectives about places and their relationships to each other over time. It is an essential ingredient in the total process of educating informed [U.S.] citizens. (24, Preface)

Figure 1.1
Integrating Geography
Across the Curriculum

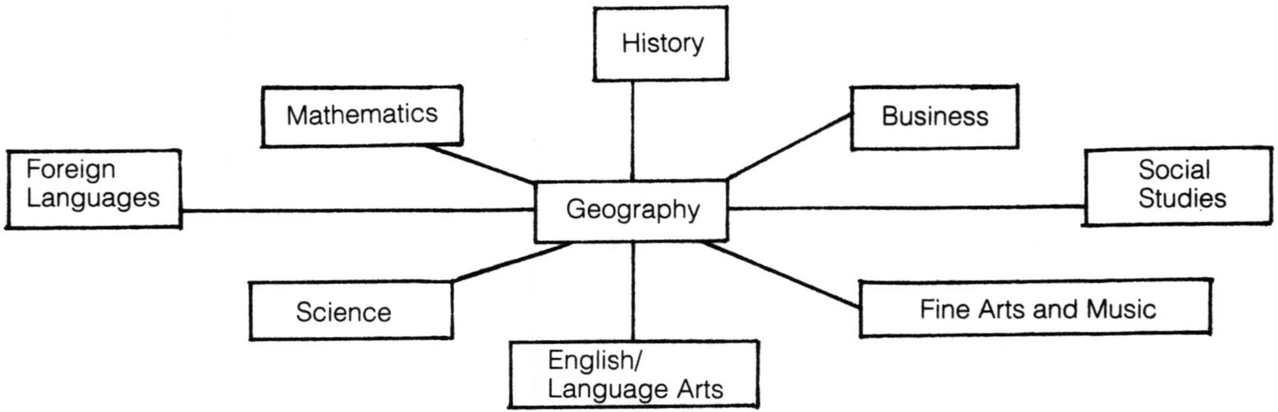

Chapter 2

CONTEMPORARY GEOGRAPHY

WHAT IS GEOGRAPHY?

Before we can consider the importance of geography's contribution to general education or the actual teaching of geography, a working definition must be established. Over its long development, and as an academic discipline, geography is not and has not remained static. It has taken on many meanings and given rise to as many misconceptions. Today these misconceptions still exercise a major influence over popular attitudes about geography and its importance, or lack thereof, to the well-rounded person.

To many people, geography conjures up memories from their own school years of rote learning of massive numbers of facts about different places and their inhabitants. Essentially, the various "tests" and "polls" that have been administered to students and young adults in the past decade have reflected the degree of mastery of this almost encyclopedic knowledge. In addition, the poor test results have been interpreted as revealing an appalling lack of understanding on the part of students about the world around them. Yet, many of these exercises are unreliable in determining the true state of "useful geographic knowledge" possessed by students upon completion of their schooling (46). This contention in turn has spawned a growing controversy among educators, community leaders, and parents not only over the value of geography, but also, more specifically, over what "kind" of geography is important to general education.

Part of the basis for this controversy is rooted in the second popular conception about geography—its relationship to discovery and travel.

17

Over the centuries a large body of literature has chronicled real and fictitious expeditions, journeys, and adventures such as those of Marco Polo and Lewis and Clark or Gulliver and Captain Kirk. A third view associates geography with maps, their creation, interpretation, and use. While all these perceptions reflect the evolution of geography as a disciplined body of thought, and to a greater or lesser extent are valid and encompassed in a modern definition of geography, there is much more.

The first significant contributions to the development of geography were made by ancient Greek and Roman scholars such as Herodotus (c. 485–425 B.C.) and Strabo (65 B.C.–20 A.D.), who wrote topographical accounts of places in their world, describing and explaining geographical phenomena and placing events in geographical perspective. The term "geography" was first used by the scholars at the great museum and library at Alexandria in the fourth century B.C. Ptolemy (90–168), working in Alexandria, considered the importance of maps and offered instructions on how to draw them in his multivolume *Geographia*. During the Middle Ages and the Renaissance the ancient tradition was carried forward by major Muslim geographer-travelers such as al-Muqaddasi (945–988), al-Idrisi (1099–1180), and Ibn Khaldun (1332–1406), among others, ushering in the great age of Western discovery. The Enlightenment brought structure and order to the field. But only in the nineteenth century did it become an institutionalized academic discipline with the founding of professional geographic organizations such as the British Royal Geographical Society in 1830, which was influenced by the development of modern science.

Contemporary geography emerges from this diverse historical process of maturation as the systematic study of the "interaction of people and environments" (12, p. 6). "Geographical training should develop the ability to 'see geographically' to observe and interpret a natural or cultural landscape in the field and/or through the study of maps, aerial photographs, and other visual representations" (25, p. 2). Consequently, the *region* as delineated by some human and/or physical uniformity is the basic unit of study, and the multidisciplinary nature of geographical analysis makes geography a bridge between the arts and the sciences (12). "Thus geographic education requires knowing *where* things are located, but more importantly requires a system for inquiring *why* they are there and where they should be" (24, p. 2).

In addition, geography is a mode of scientific inquiry through which we gain an understanding of *how* and *why* the world can support its people now and in the future. We live in a time of instant communication with film footage on television from India, Germany, Israel, etc. A global perspective is essential as our world continues to get smaller in time and space. It no longer takes weeks or months for news to travel across the oceans. As events unfold, they are televised via satellites. It is this multidisciplinary nature that greatly facilitates the integration of geography into the school curriculum for the teaching of "useful geographic information." Geography can be the framework for studying and learning about the world (14).

THE IMPORTANCE OF GEOGRAPHY TO GENERAL EDUCATION

Geography, then, is the systematic study of the interaction of people and environments as revealed in the character of specific locations or regions. And it is in its "distinctive focus upon the *study of place*" and spatial relationships that its role in general education lies. For example, in a general education setting geography poses several unique questions:

- Where is this place? (Location—the latitude, longitude gives its global address)
- What is this place like, and why does it differ from or resemble other places? (Place—the study of historical and cultural features)
- How is this place connected with other places? (Interaction—how people respond and change the physical environment)
- How and why is this place changing? (Movement—focus on systems of transportation and communication that connect people with the environment)
- What would it feel like to be in this place? (Affective—response to the environment)

Obviously, geographic learning in this context requires more than the rote memorization of such facts as capitals, commodities, and demographics: it requires that students be taught to apply this learning (34). What is more important—knowing how to use an atlas (i.e., acquiring skills to gain knowledge) or committing to memory the fact that Ndjamena is the capital of Chad?

19

Especially at the secondary level, the teaching of application often is facilitated by the teacher's adoption of general geographical cross-curricular themes. Some typical themes might be political and economic awareness, environmentalism, development (e.g., modernization), multiculturalism, and international understanding and citizenship.

GEOGRAPHY AND THE SCHOOL CURRICULUM

To achieve these goals and to help students learn to "see" geographically, geographic education in the United States begins in kindergarten and continues to be taught through grade 12. The procedure is similar in the United Kingdom and Western Europe. Mandates have been issued from all levels to standardize the goals and terminal objectives of the curriculum and to ensure that the K–12 curriculum is "balanced" by establishing minimum levels of competency. In addition, compliance with minimum standards is generally necessary for meeting school accreditation criteria (33, 53).

The regulations and guidelines for teaching geography in the United States and Western Europe are surprisingly similar; many of the goals can be and already are achieved outside geography courses by integration into other subjects. At least on paper implementation is taking place.

The principal differences between American and European sets of standards occur in two areas. Most European countries are constructing or have already adopted a national curriculum. In the United States, the individual states generally have the final responsibility for developing the school curriculum. According to the *Guidelines* prepared by the Joint Committee on Geographic Education for elementary and secondary schools, geographic education should focus on five central themes— location, place, relationships within places and movement, and regions (24, p. 3).

The European systems traditionally place a much heavier emphasis on teaching the methodology of geography and on field work. Field work takes place outside the classroom in the school yard, neighborhood, community, and/or beyond. In the United States field work is generally synonymous with field trips that are often costly and difficult to arrange. Nevertheless, such field work or field trips are strongly encouraged as a means of diversifying instruction and stimulating student interest while acquainting students with geographic methodology.

To facilitate the presentation of the material in this publication, we offer the following general scope and sequence for geography, grades K–12. It tends to embrace an expanding horizons format, characteristic of a social studies curriculum, and is a synthesis of numerous sets of guidelines, including those of the Texas Education Agency (53) and *Guidelines for Education* (24).

Kindergarten: Identification—names, location, distance, and relative sizes
Direction—right, left, up, down, etc.
Relative location
The globe as a model
Characteristics of places

Grade 1: Identification—state and country
Characteristics of the community
Location—home, school, and community
Topography of school
Weather, seasons
The map as a representation of the local environment

Grade 2: Identification and placement on maps and globes—
  neighborhood, community, state, and country, and routes
Map keys, symbols, legends
Cardinal directions
Local landforms
Seasonal change
Interdependence with and between space

Grade 3: Relative location—community, state, and country
Comparison and contrast of environmental situation
  (urban and rural)
Intermediate directions
Map scale and grid
Compass rose
Interdependence of people in communities

Grade 4: Identification and placement of state, national, and
  global physical and political features
Regions
Adaptation to environment
Interpretation of graphic models (pictures, tables,
  graphs, etc.)
Regional concept used
Comparison of regions and people
Systems of transportation

Grade 5:   Comparison, contrast, and interrelatedness
The atlas
Latitude and longitude
Where and why relationships
Decision making and environmental and global issues

Grade 6:   Cultural geography
Demography
Historical geography
Sun-earth, human-land relationships
Trade routes
Cultural characteristics (language, nationality,
   religion, etc.)
Plotting distributions

Grade 7:   State/regional geography course (year)
Human interaction with environment
Comparative analyses of areas
Diversity of populations
Geographic elements
Resolution of problems

Grade 8:   National/continental geography course (year)

Grades 9–12:   World geography course (year)
Geographic influences on state/regional history
   (physical and cultural characteristics)
Geographic influences on national history
Geographic influences on world history
Human-environment relationships
Geography of oceans
Systematic and regional analysis
Interpretation and management of problems

From the overview presented, it is evident that there are several recurring topics presented at different grade levels. These recurring themes spiral throughout the K–12 geography curriculum.

Chapter 3

THE MAP: A TOOL
FOR GEOGRAPHIC LITERACY

THE IMPORTANCE OF MAPS

As we have indicated in the previous two chapters, maps are an intimate part of geography and geographic education. But what is a map? And why is an understanding of maps considered so crucial to getting along in the future?

Simply stated, a map is the "drawn representation of geographical space" (46). Maps comprise a powerful, widely used, complex, and little understood system of communication that is as old as the spoken word. Humanity achieved "graphicacy" well before it achieved literacy. Early humans learned to draw before they learned to write and probably to draw maps before they learned to write (42). Maps graphically convey spatial images and relationships and are the point at which art and science meet. Because maps are interdisciplinary, they can be the sources of much data and should be evaluated and taught accordingly.

Cartography, the making of maps, evolved independently among many peoples in many parts of the earth; the earliest recognizable maps date back to about 15,000 B.P. The teaching of map skills and maps as learning devices has been important since the later Renaissance. By the year 1000 the Chinese were printing maps with ink on paper and using them with early examples of magnetic compasses. Modern science and technology produce maps, charts, globes, and atlases of ever-greater accuracy and scope, leading to mass dissemination of cartographic aids and their increased accessibility. Today, we continue to map not only our own shrinking planet, but the expanding universe as well (43).

Maps are artifacts that communicate across the ages to the present:

> Maps are significant landmarks of historical development and achievement, summarizing the scientific, technological, and intellectual strengths of an era and recording the political, economic, and social values of the times in which they were created. Since the beginning of history they have been intimately involved in human development. They have helped people define who they are, where they are, and how they move about. Maps delineate physical, political, economic, and social features and depict the effect the environment has on us as well as our impact on the environment. . . . Maps also can be viewed as art, part of the wider human aesthetic experience. . . (42, p. 82)

Consequently, old maps, or good facsimiles thereof, can be invaluable to teachers of history and social studies.

And as the preceding quotation intimates, the aesthetics of maps should not be overlooked in the teaching-learning process. Art historian Rudolf Arnheim has observed that maps are "a dynamic expression of color and shape" and they provide a "luxurious enrichment" of geographical and historical data. Stressing graphic communication, Arnheim also has pointed out that the aesthetic appeal of maps is like that of paintings by encouraging the viewer to ask, "Tell me who you are and what you are like" (1).

GRAPHICACY

The use of maps emphasizes visual education and sharpens visual perception, thereby stimulating the development of the student's graphicacy (38) or communication by nonverbal, nonliterary, and nonnumerical means. Graphicacy is the embodiment of the old adage that a picture can be worth more than a thousand words. As Thomas Jefferson, himself a cartographer, once pointed out, "A map can give a better idea of a region than any description in writing" (41).

Like articulacy, literacy, and numeracy, graphicacy is essential for full productive participation in modern society, where people are confronted daily by maps, graphs, charts, and diagrams in such dispensable and inescapable forms as road maps and signs, news, weather, and business reports, educational television, and advertising. Graphicacy also is basic to computer literacy (41).

The following activity uses some of the four most common and often ignored maps in everyday life: road maps, weather maps, news maps, and advertising logos. How many people are familiar with them? How many take them and most maps for granted?

What Is a Map?

This activity introduces students at all grade levels to the complexities of maps—all that maps can tell us and how they tell us. At the same time it is an experience in problem solving, viewing the map as an artifact—what a map tells us about its creators and their environment. Since maps are nonliterary documents, it also is an exercise in "graphicacy," the interpretation of data presented in graphic form.

The only resources necessary are copies of a standard state road map for students. Teachers can readily obtain these maps free from state highway departments. The rules are simple. Students are told that they are the leaders of an extraterrestrial "greenie" expedition that has landed on a small water planet that has a high radiation count, and is orbiting a moderately sized, unimpressive yellow star. On the planet, they have found the widely scattered ruins of a long-lost civilization of which no survivors remain. All that the members of the expedition know about this civilization and its creators will be derived from the ruins and other artifacts.

Road maps are the major form of evidence discovered thus far for the leaders to consider. Using this source, the class members who function as greenie department heads have been asked to determine what they can learn about the beings who once dominated the earth. The teacher tells students that they must play the roles of greenie scientists and technicians and that all their earthly knowledge of road maps must be forgotten. For example, once the maps are distributed, the students' first tendency will be to open them, thus showing that they are still earth people, A greenie scientist, on the other hand, would examine the folded map in situ first. The teacher's role, then, is to enforce this prohibition against previous earthly knowledge and to guide the analytical interchange by pointing out what kind of knowledge the greenies do possess—the state of their science and technology. Obviously, since they have journeyed far across space and time to reach the earth, the state of their science and technology is high.

The teacher continues by asking questions and giving directions as needed. For example, the sequence of questions and directions might be as follows:

- What do you notice first about the artifact? (multiple copies)
- What else do you notice about it? (portable)
- And? (folded)
- Open the artifact.
- In opening it, what becomes apparent about the physiology of the being who employed it? (structural similarity)
- What else? (polychromatic vision)
- What do you notice now about the artifact? (color)
- What else do you notice about it? (line and form)
- What else? (organization)
- What types of symbols and conventions are used? (colors, letters, and numbers)
- How do you know? (scales, inset charts, directions)
- What is the artifact? (a map)
- What was it used for? (navigation on roads)
- How do you know? (to get from place to place)
- What does the map's function tell us about its creators? (highly mobile)
- What do the material and manufacture tell us about the map's creators? (high scientific development and state of technology)
- What level of scientific and technological development is revealed by the map? (high)
- How do you know? (use of mathematics, printing, design, etc.)
- What level of aesthetic sensibility is revealed by the map? (high)
- How do you know? (use of color, line, shape, form in design)

The teacher then tells the greenie scientists-students to take the knowledge derived from the map and construct a written sketch of its creators and their civilization. They should use only information derived from and related to the map. Students will reconvene at an appointed time with their individual sketches to formulate a combined final report.

Finally, the greenie scientists-students are given a related artifact—a weather map copied from a local newspaper—and told to analyze it in writing using the same rules they used for the road map.

PART II. INTEGRATING GEOGRAPHY INTO THE SCHOOL CURRICULUM

Part II is divided into the following broad-field subject areas: history, social studies, foreign languages, English/language arts, science, mathematics, business education, and fine arts. The teaching of geography is integrated into each of these broad fields. Several examples for each area provide teachers with ideas for including geographic skills and content in the existing elementary and secondary school curriculum. At the end of each area, "Your Turn" is an opportunity to apply the knowledge gained in the activities.

Part II contains several examples of ways to integrate geographic concepts, themes, and skills in elementary and secondary classrooms. The examples, as well as the bibliographic references provided, are not meant to be exhaustive, nor will these ideas be compatible with all educational programs. But they serve to illustrate ways that teachers can include dimensions of geography into their existing curriculum. The ideas presented may also serve as a springboard for modifying existing materials and curriculum. For example, *Caravans* may not be required reading in secondary English, but the concept of using a novel to embellish a particular time period, culture, society, and historical developments as a means of focusing on the geographic information presented is what is essential. The geographic information from the novel then becomes a part of learning English.

These activities can be modified to meet individual classroom requirements and student needs. Suggested locations, regions, and continents serve as a general model that can be adapted to fit specific curricular programs. Lastly, levels for using these activities are suggested, but these too can be customized to accommodate most students regardless of grade level.

Chapter 4

GEOGRAPHY AND HISTORY

Of all the subjects in the school curriculum, geography is probably most closely related to history. Geography is a major causative factor in historical development. History has even been defined by geographic determinists as nothing more than "geography over time." Classically, whereas history has posed the questions "When?" and "Why?" geography has posed the related questions "Where?" and "Why?" Moreover, according to Backler (4), geography and history also converge as they relate to five historical concepts: (1) understanding time and chronology, (2) analyzing cause and effect relationships, (3) examining continuity and change, (4) recognizing and participating in a common memory, and (5) developing historical empathy. And the disciplines actually do come together in a legitimate subfield of both—historical geography.

Historical geography is the geography of the past or geography carried back to the past. It brings together the basic questions of both disciplines in its stress on "regional effect," the environmental impact of the region on its historical development. So, for example, it is impossible to relate accurately to students the development of one of the first civilizations, such as Bronze Age Egypt, without referring to the regional effect—the impact of the Nile River coupled with the climate on Ancient Egypt. Similarly, the history of the North American Great Plains in the nineteenth century cannot be understood without reference to the topography and aridity of the region.

Maps, too, form a connective tissue between geography and history. They are important both to geographers and to historians, albeit sometimes for different yet not wholly unrelated reasons. In their teaching and their research, geographers and historians nevertheless often are map users and makers.

Because of the close relationship between geography and history, because of the often required prominence of history in the school curriculum, and because history occupies a position between the social sciences and the humanities or in both, we feel it appropriate to devote a chapter to the integration of geography into the teaching of history apart from social studies. This chapter also sets the pattern for those to follow.

American Puzzle
(Elementary)

This example integrates the teaching of geography and map skills into a lesson on American history for the lower grades. Students piece together a commercially available wooden puzzle (e.g., Playskool) of the United States. Usually, each state forms a piece of the puzzle, and the pieces and the wooden template on which they are to be placed contain graphic representations from American history. As students are working, the teacher should help them understand that, historically and geographically, the completed puzzle is a model of the United States, state by state.

The following thinking/process skills also should be emphasized:

1. The search for *patterns*.
2. The role of *trial and error* as students try to fit the pieces together.
3. The *examination/analysis* of the remaining pieces for the right shape left on the template.
4. The search for *evidence* to fit the pieces together by looking at color and line.
5. The development of a *reason* for selecting various pieces of the puzzle.
6. The examination of *context* to determine if students use the right piece in that location.
7. The *prediction* of outcome with each piece selected to fit into the puzzle.

These process skills help students work with the parts of a problem or puzzle, and encourage them to view the whole situation. When examining world problems, it is essential that students use all these skills to arrive at a possible solution.

Next, the teacher asks students to identify their home state (e.g., Texas) and to pick up that piece of the puzzle. They are then asked to describe in writing or orally its shape, size, and location in the United States. Students also should be able to tell something about their state's role in the development of the United States/Southwest because of its location—terrain, climate, neighbors, etc.

Then, the teacher has students draw their state and add at least four representations about it. Each student is to find someone else in the class who has a similar state and to list the similarities (shape, size, population, products, etc.). The lesson concludes with each student explaining to the class his/her state map as well as that of a "sister" state.

The World of the Medieval Monastery
(Secondary)

A world civilization class is directed to read the appropriate sections in textbooks, dealing with monastic life in Western Europe during the Middle Ages. Students also read all or part of Umberto Eco's mystery novel, *The Name of the Rose*, which is set in a medieval monastery. (If it is more practical, the teacher could provide students with a summary of the novel, and have the students read only appropriate passages. A student or group of students can report on this novel for the rest of the class and/or view a videotape of the movie made from the novel.) By reading and using this novel, students are asked to draw upon the research tools of reading, interpreting, and creative imagining.

The teacher asks students to assume the role of adolescents in the Middle Ages living with their families in a community at the center of which is a great monastery. They must describe in their own words what their lives are like, their values, and the day-to-day activities of themselves and their families in making a living. They must also voice their knowledge of and attitudes toward the world outside their community. What is their world view? How do they interact with the medieval environment?

Using the descriptive passages in the novel, the teacher ask students to draw maps of the monastery and the library labyrinth that is at its center. The students then use their maps to explain the daily routines common in a medieval monastery. They can check the accuracy of their maps and visions with those supplied by the author in the novel.

The Americas Turned Upside Down
(and Inside Out?) (Upper Elementary and Secondary)

At the end of a unit on American discovery, exploration, and settlement, the teacher can use this exercise to stress the importance of geography in early American history. The unit has given students an understanding of the nature, course, and patterns of post-Columbian discovery, exploration, and settlement into the eighteenth century, and of its European causes and consequences.

Now, the teacher hangs a map upside down, showing the physical geography of the Western hemisphere. (A transparency can be used, and might even be preferable because not only can the map be projected upside down, but it can also be mirror-imaged.) Then the teacher poses the following general question to the class as a whole or to smaller groups to be answered orally, in writing, and/or graphically: "How would the early discovery, exploration, and settlement of the Americas have proceeded differently if the West Coast had been the East Coast and/or the northern and southern continents had been in inverted positions?"

Specific factors to consider among others are

1. The scarcity of good harbors on the "new" East Coast.

2. No opening into the Caribbean Sea in the east.

3. The presence of a real Northwest Passage (i.e., Straits of Magellan).

4. The presence of massive mountains ranges with few good passes like the Rockies and the Andes just beyond the East Coast.

5. The presence of hostile deserts and jungles on the other side of the mountains.

6. Less friendly Native Americans along the new East Coast.

Clearly, the discovery, exploration, and settlement of the Americas from east to west would have been far more difficult and significantly different.

Then, the teacher poses another question, "What would have been the effect of this new pattern of American discovery, exploration, and settlement on Europe?" Some possibilities to consider might be the following:

1. Would the more difficult access to and through the new East Coast to the Amerindian, animal, and agricultural wealth of the interior have led to the retarded development of Spain, France, and England?

2. Would the prominence of Russia in the North Pacific Basin and Portugal and Holland in the Indian Ocean and the easier access to and through the new West Coast have led to the greater dominance of these countries in modern European history and to Russian, Portuguese, and/or Dutch Americas?

3. Given the geographic hostility of the new East Coast, would a Northwest Passage have led to a west-to-east pattern of American discovery, exploration, and settlement? And with what consequences for Europe?

Your Turn

Interview the great African adventurer, Henry Morton Stanley, who found Dr. Livingston and first explored the Congo River. Prepare the questions you plan to ask him and write the responses.

1. What did you know of Central Africa before you first went there?
   a.
   b.
   c.

2. Where did you learn about it?
   a.
   b.

3. Why did you go?
   a.
   b.

4. What type of maps did you use, and how accurate were they?
   a.
   b.
   c.

5. How did you stay on course?

6.

7.

8.

9.

10.

Chapter 5

GEOGRAPHY AND SOCIAL STUDIES

Geography is a social science: in the school curriculum it often is included as part of the social studies. It is therefore relatively easy and quite natural to integrate the teaching of geography into the teaching of social studies. But while geography is both compatible and supportive, as the following examples illustrate, it also can effectively lead the way in conveying social studies content and analytical and other methodological skills.

Developing Map Skills
(Primary Grades)

When children come to school, they have a "wide range of incidental and systematic information about geography" (24, p. 10). This prior knowledge can be helpful in developing geographical inquiry skills. According to Forsyth (15), one means of teaching place location geography in the primary grades is through general physical exploration combined with map study. Early on, students are taught ways to develop cognitive maps of the environment (e.g., going from home to school). They develop cognitive map skills through discovery and exploration of and movement within their environments. The more traditional approach used to teach the location of places through memory work, however, is often referred to as "elaborative rehearsal" (e.g., correlating the name of a country like Italy with its unique shape).

By creating maps and models of their immediate environments as well as of their personal experiences, students put to use information they already have. One beginning activity involves students in place location exercises by having them make their own "human maps" (15). The actual map is simulated by having each student represent an object in a specific location of paths, floral scents, boundaries, etc., in their own classroom. By creating a human map students are involved in "locating" particular points in their immediate living space to guide other students through the classroom and/or school campus.

Another way to foster location learning is to have students "travel" or go on a "guided tour" (19). This "simulated" travel is complete with audiovisual materials and map references. Such experiences encourage students to use and integrate geographic information.

While reading the book *My First Day at School* by P. K. Hallinan (Ideals Publishing Corp., Nashville, Tennessee, 1989), the teacher shows the route the student in the story followed to get to school by calling particular attention to the landmarks along the way, such as the school bus, the bus stop, the street signs. The teacher also uses the cardinal directions to locate common landforms and a map of the classroom drawn to scale as a model to find items in the room. In addition, snapshots of the classroom can be used with the map to demonstrate how the same place can be shown differently.

The teacher creates the purpose of the travel by posing some type of task, such as naming three things seen on the way home or finding the quickest and/or easiest (as well as safest) way home from school. The story provides the introduction to the location exercises. Then students create their own maps to their homes, using symbols to show prominent landmarks such as houses, commercial buildings, and parks. If possible, they draw the maps to scale and then list each item shown. After creating the maps and writing the positional statements, each student shows his/her map and tells the class about the trip to and from school.

Students who complete this task are ready to create a map of a larger area, demonstrating the interaction between their homes and/or the school and the community. For example, they might draw maps showing the route to a relative's house. This map should have more detail—more symbols for different landmarks. Starting students early to develop cognitive maps as "travelers" provides intrinsic motivation to participate in trips into the community and around the state, region, and country.

Location Geography
(Middle School)

A major premise for teaching geography is to foster learning about the world around us and, more specifically, about one's own community and its diversity. Appreciating different cultural groups helps to distinguish them from each other. Each group may have its own language, customs, and forms of social and economic organization. One way to initiate such a study is by examining local settlement patterns, business types, and recreation forms. To become acquainted with different cultural groups locally, students can first focus on the downtown area of their community (if a downtown area is not available, identify one that is close to them). It is not uncommon to find groups clustered in specific areas with ethnic businesses such as restaurants, grocery stores, and import-export houses. These establishments reflect the cultural ties to the homeland of the ethnic cluster. One way to help students appreciate these connections is by doing a lesson on ethnic restaurants (16). This provides students with the opportunity to study ethnic diversity by exploring the connections between food, culture, and geography.

The teacher distributes base maps of the downtown area of a specific city where most of the restaurants are located. Several copies of the telephone directory listings of restaurants according to ethnic cuisine, or similar materials obtained from the chamber of commerce or visitor's bureau, also are distributed. The teacher then presents some general background information about the different ethnic groups that have settled in the community. The discussion focuses on customs, language, dress, music, etc.

To associate the people with their countries, the teacher uses a world map on which students locate the native lands represented by the restaurants. Using the base maps, students work in groups of three or four to create ethnic thematic maps by plotting the location of as many restaurants as possible.

Using the addresses provided in the yellow pages and other materials, students practice finding each restaurant on their maps. They mark each location with some devised symbol, perhaps a national flag, to represent the cuisine of the restaurant. After locating all the restaurants, students develop a chart, showing the connection of each restaurant with a specific country (e.g., China), region (e.g., Caribbean), and/or city (e.g., Paris). Then, on the world map, they indicate the country/region/city of origin.

Through this type of activity, students also can explore the ethnic diversity of their own class as a microcosm of the American nation. Dade County, Florida, for example, has over 100 nationalities represented among its 266,000 K–12 student population (37).

Then, building on the previous activities, students use the yellow pages again, but this time to list local businesses. Students must identify the international connection of each business, based on its name or product (e.g., Volkswagen). Once the international connections have been made, students locate the countries of origin on the world map with product symbols (e.g., cars). As a closure to the lesson, students analyze the information displayed on the world wall map.

Nationalism, National Stereotypes, and Geography
(Secondary)

A world history class is studying the development of modern nationalism and the nation state system. The teacher provides information to help students arrive at and understand the definitions of nation, nationalism, and nation state. For example, it is pointed out that at the core of the nation is a common cultural experience based upon a common language. A nation state also is defined by cultural and/or natural boundaries. Nationalism is identification with the uniqueness of that nation.

Then the teacher tells students to clear their minds and to be prepared to tell the class the first person, real or fictional, who comes to mind after he/she says the next word—for example, "American." Student responses are recorded on the board; they range from George Washington, Thomas Jefferson, John Kennedy and Martin Luther King, Jr., to John Wayne, Clint Eastwood and Michael Jackson. The teacher then helps students determine what these people have in common. For example, they are all male, English native-speakers, and are perceived as courageous, right-thinking individuals like the numerous cowboys Wayne, Eastwood, and others have played in the movies. From seeking out the common denominators, a national stereotype emerges that, while not wholly accurate, is generally believed to be so. It is therefore a reflection of the American self-image and American nationalism; it does embody a good deal of what America is about.

The teacher then asks students to determine the geographical bases for the stereotype. The physical vastness of the American experience—the frontier, for example—is a key factor in the formation of the American nation. It is at the foundation of American freedom and individualism. Hence the cowboy type as national hero. America's natural riches and isolation from the rest of the world also need to be considered.

To help students apply their learning, the teacher gives another word—"Germany," "Soviet Union," "China," or "South Africa." This time the analysis can be even more fun and complicated because the American stereotype of the country mentioned can be compared and contrasted to the actual nation or nation state. Again, geography (e.g., the Rhine as natural boundary) can be an important key to understanding.

Your Turn

Play the role of an official greeter from your community (e.g., Boston, Massachusetts). Your assignment is to welcome foreign dignitaries who are visiting the United States for the first time to gain an understanding of the workings of local government. The leaders are from Brazil. How would you make them feel welcome and facilitate their visit?

1. Welcome them in English and with some Portuguese phrases.

2. Plan an itinerary of typical local sights.

    a.

    b.

    c.

    d.

    e.

    f.

3. Explain your local governmental system.

    a.

    b.

    c.

    d.

4. Compare it to other American forms and to those of Brazil.

    a.

    b.

    c.

5.

6.

Chapter 6

GEOGRAPHY AND FOREIGN LANGUAGES

Geography is readily integrated into the teaching of foreign languages. As an essential component of the "culture track" of foreign language education, it locates and helps to define the nation and people (e.g., the Soviet Union) of the language being studied; also it often provides much of the scenery of national literature (e.g., the Caucasus Mountains of *A Hero of Our Time*). Geography contributes to the process of immersion by bringing a familiarity to language study that makes the subject matter both less formidable and more alive.

Spanish Around the World
(Secondary)

In a Spanish class, the teacher wishes to emphasize the culture of several Spanish-speaking countries. To stimulate dialogue, the teacher shows slides taken in these countries. The slides focus on the landscape, the people, markets, festivals, and the places where people live, to give students some idea of what life is like in these countries.

Each student selects one of the countries where Spanish is spoken (e.g., Spain, Mexico, Argentina) and prepares to be a tour guide in that country. In this role, students should be able to tell visitors about the local culture (landmarks, cathedrals, ruins, architectural designs) in the country. To prepare for their role, students write a script that they will use as they escort visitors to various points of interest. As an added touch, students should include phrases, words, numbers, etc., in the language of the country, using the correct accent.

In groups of three, with each student representing a different country, they identify similarities as well as differences among the countries they have researched, despite the common language. In their discussion, it is essential that students take note of the Spanish linguistic cultural similarities as well as of the differences in national cultures.

To conclude the activity, students present their findings to the entire class. One significant point to make might be that there is a strong Amerindian influence in Mexico, a strong European influence in Argentina, and a strong Moorish influence in Spain.

Pen Pals
(Elementary)

To initiate a discussion on the study of other cultures and languages, the teacher, using Spanish, for example, introduces the alphabet and proceeds to write the sounds on the chalkboard. Using a choral approach, the teacher asks students to pronounce the letter in Spanish and to spell it (e.g., *W* is pronounced "doh-bleh-vay" or "do-blehoo"). To become better acquainted with the alphabet, students then sing the letter in Spanish. Next, the teacher introduces the numbers and colors in Spanish and the class plays a form of "Concentration" to help students learn. Basic words (e.g., cat, *gato;* egg, huevo; farm, *finca)* and phrases are introduced. Then, students, on two teams, play a version of "Win, Lose, or Draw" using cards containing words in English with their Spanish counterparts. Students try to guess the word while the teacher acts as emcee, timekeeper, and scorekeeper (31).

Next, students select a pen pal from several choices. They write short notes to their new friends, working in pairs to gather the appropriate resources (e.g., foreign language guidebooks, popular magazines, foreign newspapers) to carry out the assignment. To practice forming the correct words in the language they are studying, students use pasta letters. Once they become proficient in forming words in this way, they form phrases and then sentences. Helpful information to practice with the pasta letters might include:

1. Students' age
2. A description of where they live and their daily activities.
3. A description of hobbies, sports, and other interests.
4. A description of what they look like.

Then, students get ready to travel to see their pen pals by completing a "passport application." In doing so, they find out about the rules and regulations concerning inoculations and travel restrictions. To prepare for the visit, they learn at least three traditional songs and dances of the country. In addition, they review the major historical events that have shaped its culture, language, and current societal mores and values. Next, students become familiar with the monetary units used by referring to the exchange rate published in the local U.S. newspaper. They become proficient in determining the cost of clothes, furniture, and foodstuffs in order to go "shopping" in the classroom using the currency of the country. To conclude the activity, students share with classmates their purchases as well as their learning by speaking in the language of the country.

Animals and Plants of Other Lands
(Middle School)

The study of indigenous animals and plants of French Polynesia is the focus of a French language class to illustrate that French is spoken around the world. Since the class has concentrated on France and the French spoken there, it should be interesting to look at another area of the world many miles away from France whose language is also French. Animals and plants indigenous to the islands provide the context for learning French and about French Polynesia. Students recall the names of familiar animals and plants, and an overview of the area using slides, records, and pictures is presented.

Once students are somewhat acquainted with the type of climate, the terrain, the dwellings, and the terminology used to identify them, they are ready for an in-depth study of the many indigenous animals and plants of the area. They comb through many resources to find out more about these organisms—their names, habitats, food requirements, natural shelters, and predators. As part of their investigation, students write questions on index cards about these organisms, using the correct spelling and pronunciation. On the back of the cards, they answer the questions. The cards will be used as part of an "Animal and Plant Trivial Pursuit" game to be played after each student completes at least 10 index cards with the questions and answers.

Next, students make a geographic language booklet. Using French, they describe why these species are indigenous to this particular geographical location. In addition, they explore the interaction between these animal and plant species and humans. Finally, students collect recipes in French that use these plants and animals to include in their booklets. The study of plants and animals indigenous to French Polynesia ends with a social, the "French Food Carnival," with students preparing typical dishes of the islands, using their recipes. Their booklets end with pictures of several of the animals and plants, along with photos taken at the carnival.

Your Turn

The "traveler" is going to take a trip around the world to investigate firsthand the relationship between a particular geographic area and the language that is spoken there. Also, if a language is spoken in several areas, the traveler is to take special note of the words used in each location for the same object, animal, event, etc. To prepare for this exploration of location as a determiner of language, the following questions will be helpful.

1. How does the language reflect the culture?
    a.
    b.

2. What are the basic language families, and how are they similar and/or different?
    a.
    b.

3. How are languages spread beyond the boundaries of their mother countries?
    a.
    b.
    c.

4. Using oral language, how do cultures communicate happiness, sadness, love, joy, dislike? What words and expressions are used?
    a.
    b.
    c.

5. What is the root of the contemporary language of the country you are visiting?
    a.
    b.
    c.

Lastly, the travelers keep a diary of their experiences, using a language other than English.

Chapter 7

GEOGRAPHY AND ENGLISH/LANGUAGE ARTS

The emphasis in the English/language arts curriculum is communication. Language is a tool for expressing ourselves and conveying ideas to others by speaking and/or writing. The four basic skill areas developed in this curriculum are writing (encoding), reading (decoding), speaking (encoding), and listening (decoding). Literary appreciation and criticism are also emphasized.

English/language arts is taught in a variety of ways to help students learn the skills and tools of communication. Most skills are sequenced and spiral throughout the grades. Students must have opportunities to practice language arts skills whether speaking before their peers, engaging in drama or group activities, writing letters, listening to a poem, or watching a video. These skills are interrelated: language is received and decoded or expressed and encoded. The examples that follow illustrate the interrelatedness of the language arts and provide contexts for integrating geography into the instruction.

When working on the mechanics of written communication, language use, and vocabulary development, students learn the skills related to informational writing, letter writing, and creative writing. But how can we get students to write and at the same time improve their writing skills? According to McNergney and Haberman (32), the sharing of ideas with others, i.e., writing, begins with real-life topics. Also, in real life we write to people of our choosing. As McNergney and Haberman point out, in school students write for teachers and for a grade. But students need a context in which to write and their writing skills should be used outside of school as well as inside. Their audience should be specific and so should their purpose.

The Geography of a Novel
(Secondary)

When students read a novel, a play, or a poem in an English class, geographic themes can be emphasized. For example, Davenport (13) used James Michener's *Caravans* to help his students learn about the geography, the people, and the culture of this remote region of the world (South Central Asia—specifically Afghanistan). Students are introduced to "the geographic elements" and facts about Afghanistan while reading Michener's novel. To some, it is like reading the *National Geographic* without pictures.

In addition to reading the novel for its storyline and characters, *Caravans* can be read for its geographic content by emphasizing the following:

1. Landscape—physical as well as human, including climate, vegetation, drainage, topography, cities, villages, and farms.

2. Human ecology—the human relationship to the land and its influence on the quality of life.

3. Economics—the way people make a living, the communication and transportation systems, and the products produced.

4. Regionalism—the reflection of the area uniformity as defined by the physical and/or human cultural characteristics (Lamme in Davenport [13]).

To better understand such physical elements as the climate of Afghanistan, comparisons can be made between South Central Asia and the American Southwest—Texas, for example. Climate determines where and how people live, the types of transportation routes, the way people spend leisure time, and decisions regarding land use (24). In the novel, *Caravans*, the human element is exemplified by the nomads and their seasonal migration routes as related to the climate and the availability of pastureland for their flocks. When Davenport (13) followed the seasonal migration patterns based on the information in the text, he found an apparent contradiction in the annual route of Kocki. The use of films, too, can be helpful, "to provide pictorial reinforcement of images created by [the] prose" (13, p. 263). Salter and Lloyd (47) advocate using literary settings and characters to encourage greater sensitivity to geographical space. The author's treatment of the landscape and personal space helps to link the reader with the physical and cultural geography of the location.

In this activity the teacher uses a literary work as a tool to integrate the study of world history and contemporary literature with geographic content. Students engage in an in-depth examination of Afghanistan, the description of the people, their country, and their way of life. Using the storyline in

Caravans, for example, and maps, students have an opportunity to learn about people who are thousands of miles away. Geographic knowledge about a new culture and way of life helps students understand who they are and by studying about where Afghans live, they learn why they live there and how geography influences their lives.

Once students locate and describe places on a map of South Central Asia, the information in the novel comes alive and they can plot the migration routes that the nomads took to feed their families and animals. They become familiar with the names of the mountain ranges, major cities, ideal places to graze animals, the daily tasks of family members, and the foods served during the course of a day.

To extend the technique of geographic inquiry, along with developing writing skills, students pretend they are newspaper reporters and plan a trip to Afghanistan. Since the war with the Soviet Union has ended, Michener's Afghanistan is very different from the country today. All reporters should be prepared to face a country ravaged by war and should have information about the following:

1. The major economic centers and their historical significance (they develop a report)

2. The inoculations they will need in order to travel

3. The clothes they will need (they generate a list)

4. The transportation routes they will take once they are in the country (they prepare a travel itinerary for internal travel).

In addition, the reporters should prepare sets of questions to ask the men, women, and children they will meet to write the story, "Now That the War Is Over."

Semantic Mapping
(Elementary and Middle School)

After the teacher presents the basic skills regarding punctuation, capitalization, sentence structure, word usage, and style, students need a beginning point to get ready to write about something meaningful to them. Many approaches can be used; the semantic map is one. This strategy can be used as a way to generate ideas for writing and to put to use many of the language skills that have been taught. The ideas to use in the semantic map can come from reading stories in the basal reader, newspaper and magazine articles, and personal reading.

If, for example, the class was preparing for Earth Day and students were adding articles about the greenhouse effect, acid rain, and/or the tropical rain forest to the current events bulletin board, the students may want to write about one or all of these topics. For illustrative purposes, let's use the tropical rain forest as the subject of student interest.

Students develop a semantic (or spider) map. Such a map conveys the key aspects and relationships of a concept in picture form. An activity using a semantic map provides a graphic representation that generates ideas. The map offers a context for associations and assists students in practicing language skills, recalling information related to the key concepts, interpreting data, making analogies, comparing and contrasting ideas, and classifying terms.

Students write the concept *tropical rain forest* in the middle of a sheet of paper, draw lines outward from the concept, and add information at the ends of these lines (see Figure 7.1).

Next, as they think about the tropical rain forest, students answer the following questions, based on the five themes of geography.

1. Where is this place?

2. Why is this place like, and why does it differ from or resemble, other places?

3. How is this place connected to other places, systems, and people?

4. How and why is this place changing?

5. What would it feel like to be in this place?

As students answer these questions, they add more information to their maps. Once they have responded to the questions, they share their maps with their neighbors. Using a second color pen/pencil, each student adds the newly shared information to his/her individual map. After the sharing, students view the 6.5-minute videotape *Rain Forest Rap* (55). Then they draw conclusions about the tropical rain forest. Students are refining their listening skills because much valuable information about the forest is presented in a very short time. Lastly, individually or in small groups, students look at their own maps and create a second map, categorizing and sequencing the material scattered on the original. If they are working in groups, they discuss ways to classify their information.

Students apply the information they have gained about the tropical rain forest and the writing skills they have acquired by assuming the role of a Sierra Club member who is concerned about the destruction of this valuable biome in Central and South America. They select one of the following tasks:

1. Plan a letter-writing campaign to Washington and to the United Nations to make world leaders aware of this concern (using punctuation and capitalization skills, etc.)

46

Figure 7.1
Semantic Map of the Tropical Rain Forest

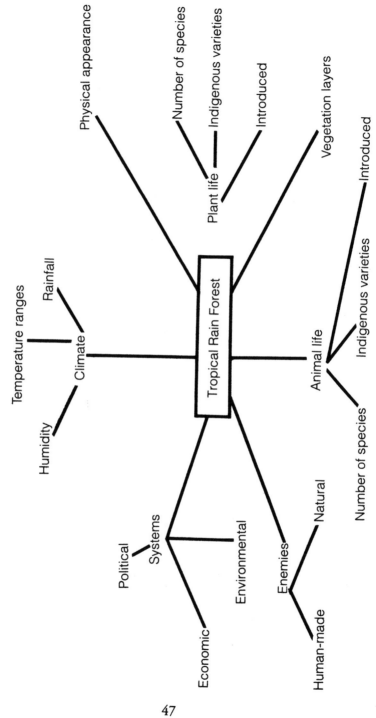

2. Plan a conference to examine the problem from a global perspective.

   a. To be one of the speakers, they must write a speech.

   b. Format?

3. Develop a survey instrument for students and teachers to complete.

   a. Draft a sample questionnaire using correct grammar.

   b. Tabulate the results.

   c. Determine how the results will be used.

4. Collect, read articles and books, and outline each of the major points dealing with the impact of the destruction of the rain forests.

   a. Global warming?
   b. Economic benefits and/or drawbacks?

5. Identify two other examples in history analogous to the destruction of the rain forests and write a position paper that represents your feelings about the issue.

6. Read *Journey Through a Tropical Jungle* by Adrian Forsythe (Simon and Schuster, 1986). Then, use this book as one of the guides on the trip through the Monteverde Cloud Forest in Costa Rica. Take notes about specific animals and plants you encounter so that you can share your odyssey with others. Using these examples, be prepared to defend why these areas need to be preserved.

Nature and Language Arts
(Elementary and Middle School)

Vocabulary knowledge is essential if students are to understand the meaning of individual words and then put them together into a meaningful whole as they read for comprehension (26). In the Nature Walk exercise, it is hoped that students will (1) learn new vocabulary words; (2) learn the meaning of these new words; (3) be able to select pictures that will illustrate each word (or draw one); and (4) be able to use the vocabulary in the appropriate context when writing a haiku. In addition, they will be practicing dictionary skills by putting vocabulary sheets in alphabetical order as well as developing their reading skills as they read the class book that contains all the vocabulary sheets.

The Nature Walk exercise illustrates one way to identify vocabulary words and use them in a specific context. As students walk along, they will have concrete examples to which they can refer to illustrate the meaning of a word. Also, the nature walk brings the life in school—learning communication skills—a little closer to the world they live in—their natural environment. Students do not just memorize words, they learn new words and their meanings through meaningful experiences.

The teacher takes students on a nature walk to a large wooded area not far from the school. The area was selected because the owner, who originally said the property would become part of a city park, now wants to sell it to a developer. Sale of the property will require a zoning change. The teacher prepares students for the walk, suggesting that the area may not look the same in three years. He/she emphasizes the physical features of the land, the plants and animals living there, as well as its aesthetic contribution to the surrounding community. In the classroom, slides of the area are also shown.

The objective of the nature walk is not only to become aware of the physical environment, but to increase vocabulary. Students are to develop a geographical dictionary, using the information they collect on the nature walk. To help them remember what they see and hear, they record data on a chart similar to the one given in Figure 7.2. While still in the classroom, using one example provided, students enter the information under the appropriate category on their charts. Then they take their walk, after which they return to the classroom.

Students identify the geographical terms on their charts and print or write each one neatly on a blank sheet of paper, leaving room for operational definitions and illustrations. Then, working in small groups, they alphabetize the sheets. If they do not know the definitions, they can construct "word maps." They answer three questions: (1) What is it? (2) What is it like? (3) What are some examples? (26). Next they look through magazines for pictures they can use to illustrate the terms. If they cannot find appropriate illustrations, they can draw them. At the end of this activity, students have a geographical word bank, containing new terms and definitions. As they build their word bank, they expand their geographical knowledge and their vocabularies.

To apply their knowledge of these geographical terms, students write a haiku, a three-line nonrhyming poem. For example,

> The hill is golden, (5 syllables)
> And the wind is cold and damp, (7 syllables)
> So it must be fall. (5 syllables)

All students' pages, complete with terms, definitions, illustrations, and haiku are placed in a class book. One by one, each student reads his/her page, as classmates listen and count the number of syllables in the haiku.

Figure 7.2
Findings from Nature Walk

Animals Living There	Plants Living There	Places They Live	Food They Eat	Type of Land	Type of Soil	Climate/ Temperature	Other

Your Turn

As part of a unit on nineteenth century British literature, ask students to read Robert Louis Stevenson's popular swashbuckling adventure novel, *Treasure Island* (1883). As background to the book, present information about the British Empire in the early eighteenth century, its rivalries with Spain and France, and the role of privateering (piracy) in these relationships. Discuss the example of the infamous Captain Kidd and his "lost" treasure.

Based on information supplied in the novel, students become map readers and makers.

A. On a world map students try to trace the route to Treasure Island from England

    1. Cardinal direction(s)

      a.

      b.

    2. Location of Treasure Island

      a. Caribbean Sea?

      b. South Pacific Ocean?

      c.

B. Students draw the map of Treasure Island described in the book.

    1. Location of cove where ship was moored?

    2. Fort?

    3. Ben Gunn's cave?

    4. Treasure?

    5.

    6.

    7.

C. How can students be motivated to apply their geographic and map skills after reading this book?

    1. Compare old and new maps of the regions traversed in the book.

    2. What are the possible destinations for Long John Silver?

    3. Compare the possible journey of Silver with the actual one made by Captain Bligh after being set adrift by the mutineers in *Mutiny on the Bounty*.

    4.

    5.

    6.

D. How would you extend this lesson into one focusing on writing?
Drama? Art?

  1. Writing
     a.
     b.
     c.

  2. Drama
     a.
     b.
     c.

  3. Art
     a.
     b.
     c.

  4.

  5.

  6.

Chapter 8

GEOGRAPHY AND THE ARTS

Geography is a viable inroad into the world of the arts. As with other subject areas, geography can locate the arts. In music, geography can provide part of the background for a particular composer and his work (e.g., Sibelius' "Finlandia") or the natural setting for folk music (e.g., the Blue Ridge Mountains). Knowledge about the South Seas can give students an additional insight into Gauguin's painting. And the physical environment often helps to determine the character of folk art, as in the case of the materials, coloration, and decoration of African or Central American Indian textiles. Musical selections can provide aesthetic awareness of land and seascapes, climate conditions, historical events, and national and political cultures (54). Thus the integration of geography into music and art education and art history can give students a deeper appreciation for the subject matter, human situations, and individual works of art.

International Design
(Elementary)

The teacher introduces students to the country of Japan (or any other country of interest) with an explanation of its history and culture. To facilitate students' understanding, slides, filmstrips, short films, maps, and other audiovisuals can be used. Students also can read stories telling how children grow up in Japan. They can even learn some basic Japanese words, phrases, and customs such as taking off one's shoes before entering a home. They can be taught a traditional song, such as "Haru Ga Kite," sung to welcome the flowers and birds of spring (*Raffi Everything Grows Songbook* [New York: Crown Publishers, 1989]).

Once students have had a good introduction to Japan, the teacher asks each one to create a flag for the country, using crayons, colored pencils, paints, and paper, cutting up pieces of colored paper and pasting them together, or combining various techniques. When all the flags have been completed, the teacher asks each student to show his/her flag to the class and explain the meaning of the color, shapes, and images used. But before they make these presentations, the teacher shows and explains the real Japanese flag as an example.

Students are then asked to make a collage-mural about Japan (its geography, culture, dress, etc.) on a large continuous piece of paper to introduce students and teachers from other classes to this fascinating country. Once the mural is completed, students can take turns as tour guides explaining it to classroom visitors. In addition, they can serve Japanese green tea and play the music from lutes (*biwa* and *shamisen*) to create the appropriate atmosphere to complement the tea ceremony.

Music of the World
(Elementary)

The teacher can use the same kind of introduction for this activity as that used in the preceding example, adding representative traditional music, dance, and drama of the country. Viewing a tape or film of a short Kabuki performance would be helpful for Japan, for example.

Students can practice what they are learning about the arts of the country by singing basic songs and/or by doing simple dances. In the process they also can make costumes to help them better understand the meanings of their performances.

Then, students can view a film or a tape of a folk dance and accompanying music from a distant but related area (e.g., Fiji or Hawaii, in the case of Japan). Have them note and demonstrate the similarities (e.g., expressiveness of the hands in portraying wind, rain, sunshine) and differences (e.g., rhythms) between this music and dance and that of the original country.

Another use of music, related by Kracht (29), is to have students explore the musical expression of the environment in sea chanties by reading original sources such as letters from old-time mariners. Using these sources, students also can trace the voyages described on a map.

National Currency and Stamps, Geography, and Art (Secondary)

The assignment for a secondary art class is to design a new national paper currency for the United States that reflects not only something of its history, but also something of its natural wonders. Students view examples of existing currencies from around the world (Cayman, Canadian, Dutch, Chinese) that show the country's geography. They are told to pay attention to the use of color and other factors of design, as well as to the portrayal of geography.

Then each student is asked to design a particular denomination, creating an obverse and reverse of a new bill in full color. When completed, each student explains to the rest of the class the significance of the colors, symbols, representations, etc., in his/her bill.

Students are then asked to apply what they have learned by designing a postage stamp, commemorating an aspect of the geography of any country of their choice outside the United States. Map stamps are acceptable. Again, upon completion, each student explains to the class his/her stamp, its content, and the techniques used to create it.

Your Turn

Acid rain is the menace of the tropical rain forest and the ancient art treasures of Southern Mexico and Central America. Archaeologists and art historians from all countries have become concerned because of the extensive damage that has occurred worldwide from Athens and the Parthenon to India and the Taj Mahal.

Chemical weathering, caused by pollutants from burning grasslands, oil refineries, and exhaust from cars and buses, has eroded facial features of stone statutes and facades of ancient buildings. What can be done to help students become aware of this destruction and also to consider ways of slowing down the process?

A. Obtain weather reports and other meteorological data from Mexico, Guatemala, Belize, Honduras, and Cuba to trace the sources of the acid rain to the areas of destruction.
   1. What are some of the sources?
      a. Uncapped Mexican oil wells
      b. Oil refinery emissions
      c.
      d.

2. What treasures are endangered? Where are they located?
   Obtain local maps.
   a.
   b.
   c.

B. How can you document the acceleration process caused by acid rain?
   1.
   2.
   3.

C. What are the political ramifications of acid rain within these countries and across the globe? Are the ancient treasures something all of us need to try to preserve? What are our responsibilities?
   1.
   2.
   3.

Chapter 9

GEOGRAPHY AND SCIENCE

Geography is often considered a science, "particularly [when] a focus on the physical aspects of the environment is strong" (p. 12). Like geology and biology, geography focuses on human activities and the earth. Clearly, these elements overlap. In addition, like the sciences, geography promotes scientific investigation, understanding, and information. Thus, it is natural to emphasize geographic concepts in various science courses.

To some degree, including current environmental and human problems in a science class helps to introduce relevant content, whether acid rain, the greenhouse effect, the tropical rain forest, or AIDS. These problems need to be solved and science will make its contribution, but geography will provide a different perspective—one of understanding and appreciation of different places and diverse societies.

Animal and Plant Diversity Around the World
(Elementary)

After reading stories about African wildlife, such as *Ogden Nash's "Zoo"* (Ray Finamore, ed. [New York: Stewart, Tabori, and Chang, 1987]), the teacher has students locate the native habitats of the animals presented in the story on a map of Africa. After a discussion about what these animals eat, the general climate, foliage, and terrain of their habitats, and other animals that share the same areas, students examine different maps, citing these data. In addition, the discussion focuses on the role of the parents, what the young learn during the early years, the natural enemies of these animals,

57

and the degree of nurturing required before the animals become independent. To find more information about these animals, students use reference materials as more questions are raised during the discussion.

Then, on a map of Africa students plot the migration routes the animals take to ensure that they have enough water and food throughout the year. Next, using different color pens, they shade in the areas of dense vegetation on one map of Africa and on another the locations of the wildlife reserves and national forests.

Next, using an overlay technique, students discuss and analyze what the maps communicate about migration patterns of different animals, watering holes, etc. In chart form they list the animals under investigation and find out the total number of each species. Based on this information, plus that gleaned from the overlays, students determine if the animals are endangered; if so, they are to investigate the contributing factors, which they will also list on the chart (see Figure 9.1).

Figure 9.1
Animals of Africa

Animal	Total Count	Endangered	Contributing Factors

As a concluding activity, ask students to think of three ways to help stem the decline of specific animals (e.g., write to Greenpeace for literature or write a letter to legislators and community leaders protesting the killing of elephants for ivory and of leopards for their skins).

Environmental Awareness
(Elementary/Middle School)

One way to learn more about a civilization and its people might be to study its refuse. "Trashology," or the study of garbage, can be very informative. In this activity, students examine selected pieces of trash from their classroom. They are asked to recreate who might have used each item and for what purpose, using clues from the trash to draw conclusions about the activities

58

that might have occurred. Then they complete a chart (see Figure 9.2) to identify the item, its age, who might have thrown it out, the material it is made of, and any other information that might be helpful. During the discussion, specific analytical techniques are presented—the age of the material, the type of material used, addresses, if any, the order of the items in the trash receptacle, etc.

As a homework assignment, ask students to practice their inference skills by going through a trash basket at home. Using the chart created in school as a model, they complete a second one with the items found at home.

Locating the Original Homes of Fruit
(Secondary)

During a life science lesson on angiosperm plants, the product of reproduction, the fruit, is the topic of discussion. To add a geographic dimension, the places of origin of specific fruits are presented. Because bananas, peaches, apples, and other fruits, the products of sexual reproduction, have specific climatic requirements, location serves as the beginning point of this study. Using the pineapple as an example, students learn that the Hawaiian Islands are not its original home: it is a native of South and Central America and was later brought to the Islands. Students identify the regions of origin for the following:

1. Lemons
2. Blueberries
3. Apricots
4. Tomatoes
5. Grapes-Raisins

But before they can answer the question about original location, they must do some research about the fruit. For example:

1. Where is it grown now?
2. What are its climatic and soil requirements?
3. How long has it been in existence?
4. Which is the oldest known fruit?
5. What are its genus and species? Common name?
6. Was it considered a delicacy in the past? Today? Why?

59

Figure 9.2
Environment Awareness
(What Trash Tells Us)

Item	Age	Used Only Once? Recycled?	Who Used It?	Materials Made of	Domestic/ Imported	Other

Then students investigate one fruit not already researched and write its biography. To make the biography more complete, they need the following additional information:

1. Unique facts about the fruit
2. Annual production levels
3. Derivative products
4. Importance as a food product
   a. Food value
   b. Staple?

Your Turn

You have planned a unit on insects for your science classes and you want your students to become more aware of the movement of insects, particularly the movement of the killer bees during the last three decades. Of late, these bees have become an international problem involving many countries, particularly Mexico, Central and South America, and the United States. The prediction is that this variety of bees is to arrive in South Texas by the spring of 1990. To become acquainted with this topic, students investigate the following questions:

A. Where did the killer bees come from?

B. What efforts have been made to fight the invasion?
   Where did these efforts originate?
   1.
   2.
   3.

C. Why were the killer bees first in Brazil?
   1.
   2.
   3.

D. Where have the bees traveled?
   1. On a map locate the countries the bees have traveled across—replicate their migration pattern and predict where they will go after leaving Texas.
   2.
   3.
   4.

E. What are the history and behavioral characteristics of these bees, as well as their relationship to humans?
   1.
   2.
   3.
   4.

F. What is the cost to the lower Rio Grande Valley of dealing with this insect in terms of
   1. Money lost to crops?
   2. The general economy?
   3. Pollution—chemicals used to control them?
   4.

Chapter 10

GEOGRAPHY AND MATHEMATICS

A geographical format lends itself well to the teaching and/or practice of mathematical concepts and skills. Mathematical skills and understandings are an integral part of geography. When studying population and other statistical data, using problem-solving approaches to deal with global issues and computational skills to determine growth patterns, quantitative skills are practiced and applied in meaningful contexts and in purposeful ways.

Maps themselves are, of course, mathematically based. The integration of geography into the teaching of mathematics can help to provide a basis in physical and practical reality for a theoretical subject matter and thereby facilitate learning. Geography also can underscore the universality of mathematical knowledge and its interrelationships with other bodies of knowledge.

Problem Solving Using a Global Context
(Elementary/Middle School)

Given the current emphasis in mathematics on the application of computation skills in realistic situations and on problem-solving skills, human and physical geographic issues provide opportunities to achieve these mathematical goals. Whether the topic is natural resources, the environmental consequences of industrial and nuclear waste, or the effects of population or other geographic dimensions, within the context of mathematical problems these are meaningful issues for students to discuss and think about.

After the teacher presents the problem situations, students solve several problems individually or in small groups. The following might be used:

1. Looking at population growth rates for the past five years for Mexico and for such European countries as Sweden and Italy and for the United States, what will be the rate of increase for each country in the next five years? How much time will it take for the population to double? Is the population growing arithmetically or

63

exponentially? What is the population density per square kilometer? What is the per capita income?

    a. Using basic multiplication skills, students can calculate what the doubling would be and within what length of time.

    b. Finally, the teacher can initiate a discussion that focuses on population growth and its impact on the physical and human qualities of the land and the life of its people (48).

2. Another example, which is offered by Schwartz (48), deals with global hunger. Students use a variety of math skills—fractions, percents, and ratios—and at the same time consider the effects this problem has on the typical diets in Western countries. For example, if four-fifths of the grain in Canada is fed to animals, what percentage does it represent? How can land be used to grow crops for people rather than to grow crops and feed them to animals to provide meat?

Mathematics and the Census
(Elementary)

The 1990 census can be used to encourage student thinking about this procedure. The teacher presents specific information about the census. The concern for a national census goes back to the time of the framing of the Constitution. To ensure appropriate representation, the first decennial census was initiated in 1790. Although this census generated very little information, it was a beginning; today "the decennial census is limited to population and housing" (8). The following example is part of a teaching package prepared by the Department of Commerce to provide students with relevant and useful information about the census and also to provide teachers with census education materials.

Students read the story, "RIGHT + UNDER = MISSEDPOP," concerning a make-believe land that is ruled by the High Council. MISSEDPOP has two states—RIGHT and UNDER. RIGHT has 250 people and UNDER has 200 people. Over the years, RIGHT has always had more people than UNDER. The following story is taken directly from the material prepared by the Department of Commerce (Bureau of the Census, #DX-3300F, Activity 2, 1988).

Because RIGHT has more people it has more power in the High Council, with five members to UNDER'S four. Needless to say, the people of RIGHT are happy. When the council votes on things, RIGHT always seems to win. RIGHT got the new swimming pool. It got the new park. It even got the new library. The people feel their council members represent them well. They tell their council members what they need. Since RIGHT has more people, it gets more votes. Some people in UNDER feel it is unfair, but it is fair. In the law it was written, "There shall be nine members of the High Council. Their number shall be divided between the two States. This shall be done using

64

the number of people living in each. The people of MISSEDPOP shall be counted every 10 years to do this. This count shall be called a census. This count shall decide the number of members for each State."

It has been 10 years since the last census. The number of people in each State had changed. This was known. Some people had died, but many babies had been born. Some people had left MISSEDPOP. Others had moved to MISSEDPOP from faraway lands. The numbers had changed but no one knew by how much. They would soon know. The census was being taken. The leaders of UNDER thought they would finally beat RIGHT. They thought they had more people than it did. They had to prove it. The only way was to be counted. To be counted, everyone has to fill out a census form. They were then to send it to the capital of MISSEDPOP.

The leaders of RIGHT knew some people would not care about the census. They knew some new people from faraway lands would be afraid. They knew others just would not understand.

The leaders of RIGHT went everywhere in the State. They spoke to their people. They showed them the count was important. They talked about the new park, the new library, and the new swimming pool. They told the people there was nothing to fear. The people listened. Everyone from RIGHT turned in the census forms.

In the State of UNDER, the leaders did nothing. They were so sure they would be Number 1. They did not try to talk to their people. They did not see the need.

The people of UNDER are not very different from the people of RIGHT. Some of them, too, did not care to be counted. Some were afraid. Some did not understand why the census was important. So some of the people of UNDER did not answer the census.

Then, the census ended. The numbers were totaled. RIGHT had grown to 300 people. UNDER had grown too! The leaders of UNDER cheered, until they heard the number. It was 240.

The leaders of UNDER were shocked. "It has to be wrong," they said. "It has to be changed." Nothing could be done. The number was final. It would stand for another 10 years. UNDER had been undercounted.

The old council was then used. It decided the number of High Council members for each State. With 540 people in MISSEDPOP, each member of the council would stand for 60 people. With 300 people in RIGHT, it got 5 members. With 240 people in UNDER, it only got 4 members. The council had not changed. The people of UNDER who were not counted might have changed this. Alas, it was too late.

Everyone in UNDER quickly understood what those missing people meant. The very next day the High Council had a vote. It decided where to put the new school. The vote was 5 to 4. RIGHT had won again.

After students have read the story, have them work in small groups to practice what they have learned about the importance of participating in a census.

1. Students study the map provided and list what they find on the map. (See Figure 10.1.)
2. Then, they decide what other items can be added to the map; when the group members agree, they draw these on the map.
3. With input from all group members, they decide which state is bigger based on the land area of each.
4. Students calculate the population growth for each state from the last census to the present one. (On an average how many people were added to each during the past 10 years?)
5. As part of the 1990 Census in the United States, what will states do to encourage citizens to complete the appropriate forms?

Students are now ready to consider the important question based on this story. How has the average number of people represented by one council member changed in MISSEDPOP? To respond to this question, students have to apply what they have been taught about taking a census and its ramifications as reflected in making decisions for each community. The concluding question is, What impact does the census have on the political systems of MISSEDPOP and of the United States?

The International Language of Mathematics
(Middle/Secondary)

The study of mathematics as a language introduces students to the different numbering systems of the past. These systems were linked to civilizations and their written languages. The teacher presents the symbols and signs of the Egyptian, Roman, Hindu, and Arabic numbering systems and discusses how, where, and why they developed. Students begin to see the connections between numeracy and literacy in each civilization and that "language reflects culture's need." They also begin to recognize that mathematical languages have rules similar to those in English, French, German, and other spoken languages. And as in any language, symbols are combined to form larger units to communicate different numerical concepts. Today, 5,445 languages are spoken around the world (49).

Students use their understanding of language systems and computational skills to investigate further the common elements among today's languages.

1. If 250 languages are no longer spoken, how many languages were spoken at one time?
2. If India has 845 spoken languages, what fractional part of the total do they represent?

Figure 10.1
The Land of Missedpop

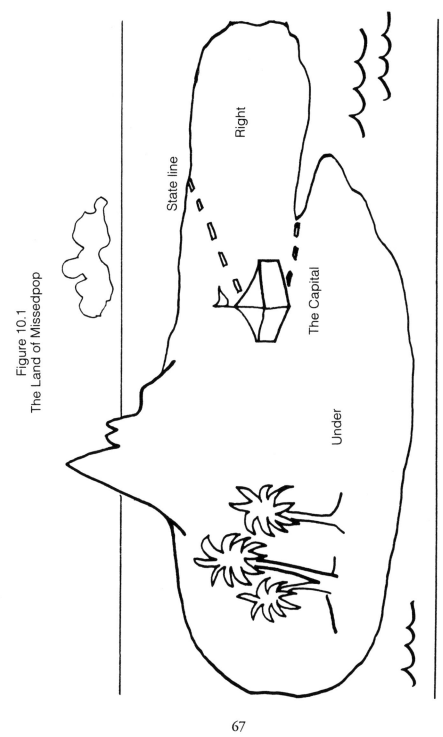

SOURCE: Department of Commerce, Bureau of the Census, DX-3300F, Activity 2, 1988.

3. English has the most technical terms of any language. If it has 790,000 words, 490,000 of which are nontechnical, how many technical terms does it have? Of this total, what percentage does the 6,000-word vocabulary of the average person represent?
4. From which old world language and country does the word "ok" come? Hint: It also has the longest term, *Kraftfahrzeugreparaturwerkstatten.*
5. Which writing system is the oldest? How old is it? Where does it come from?

Then, students research the Hindu-Arabic number system in detail. They select one whole number operation and identify the rules that govern it. Next, they compare these rules with those used to write sentences and construct paragraphs in the English language.

Your Turn

Using a facsimile map of the greater Southwest in the early eighteenth century, have students plan a trip across Spanish Texas from San Antonio de Bexar to Nacogdoches, a distance of 300 miles "as the crow flies." In 1721 a Spanish Texican could travel approximately 9 leagues a day by wagon.
A. If 1 league = 2.6 miles, how many miles does the traveler go in a day?
B. How long will it take to make the journey?
C. What points of interest will be found along the trail?
   1.
   2.
   3.
D. How long would it take to make the journey today by car at 55 mph?
E. How has the route changed in over 250 years?
   1. It is an interstate highway.
   2.
   3.
F. How has the route stayed the same?
   1. The general route is essentially the same.
   2.
   3.
G. Compare and contrast traveling by wagon and by car.
   1.
   2.
   3.

Chapter 11

GEOGRAPHY AND BUSINESS

Modern business, whether local or international, is predicated on spatial relationships and linkages. An interconnected activity, it helps to create a global community. In fact, the manufacture, distribution, buying, and selling of goods and services in the contemporary world are geographic activities. Consideration of some major ethical issues in business such as those relating to the pollution and/or desecration (e.g., strip mining) of the environment must also rest on geographic foundations. Therefore not only is it relatively easy to integrate geography into the teaching of business subjects, but to help prepare students more fully for participation in the business-oriented world of the future it is imperative that we do so.

The World in a Candy Bar
(All Levels)

The teacher begins the lesson by showing a candy bar to pique students' interests and to demonstrate how people are connected across the globe. The teacher emphasizes that people, goods, and ideas travel, often as a part of a system. Using a guided discussion approach, the teacher asks such questions as, What is a system? How many systems are there? What happens if one part of the system breaks down or stops functioning? How can the concept of systems be applied to geography? What do systems have to do with business?

Once the whole class has an opportunity to participate and listen to the various responses, students are ready to work in small groups. To put their new information about systems to work, each group is given a candy bar and the members are asked to list its main ingredients, including those in the wrapper. Using a blank world map, the group members are asked to locate the source of the ingredients, indicating the country on the map. The question is, how are these goods moved from the place of origin to the place of production? What transportation systems might be used to move the ingredients? Students in their groups talk extensively about one system— that of transporting the ingredients from where they are grown to where they are processed and become part of the candy bar.

Still working in groups, students consider how the candy-bar system is like the world food supply system, using the following questions:

1. What might cause problems in the world food supply system?
2. What happens when the world's food supply system breaks down?
3. How can we help people in other countries when there are food shortages?

As a climax to the lesson, students create a map poster, including the names of the countries and connecting (with yarn) the places of origin of the ingredients used in the candy and the production plant. Once these points have been identified with the yarn, ask students to cut one of the lines and discuss the implications when the route between origin and production is broken. What impact would the break have on the various businesses involved in the production of the candy bar? Now all are ready to enjoy eating their candy bar.

This activity was adapted from one that appears in *Teaching Geography: A Model for Action* (Washington, D.C.: National Geographic Society, 1988), which contains several other activities that teachers might find helpful.

Urban Business Geography
(Secondary)

In this activity, students learn about all the factors that business leaders consider when making a decision about where to build their companies. These include taxes, cost of land, available work force, educational opportunities, general economy, and many other considerations. Geography certainly plays a role. After an extensive introduction by the teacher, students are ready to put their knowledge to work and practice what they have just learned.

Students are to simulate the site selection process of a new computer repair business/company. Leaders of "We Fix What You Break" have organized a committee to study the issue and to identify a suitable place to build the new repair facility. Students work in small groups, each of which assumes the role of a site selection committee. First, students generate a list of resources needed to provide an efficient and profitable enterprise. This information is essential before any decisions regarding potential cities can be made.

After the lists have been generated, the class convenes to develop a comprehensive list, placing the most important resources first. Then, returning to their respective groups, students are ready to generate the type and kind of information they need to make a decision regarding the appropriate site for the repair company. Each committee receives information submitted by four different cities (see Figure 11.1) to compare and rank the cities based on this information. For each city the committees consider the following data:

1. General statistics
2. Transportation available
3. Tax base of the city/community
4. Labor force available
5. Utilities
6. School system
7. Access to other areas of the country and world

Committee members evaluate this information and make a decision. Since the citizens of these communities are anxious to know if their city was selected, each committee prepares a news release explaining what the decision will mean to the company and the community.

To extend the activity, students use maps of individual states/cities to identify a city that is similar to the one selected with regard to population, transportation, etc. To do this, they will need to examine population maps as well. As they apply what they have learned, students become convinced more than ever that they have selected the best city for the computer repair business. (This activity was modified from one that appeared in *Teach-Practice-Apply: The TPA Instruction Model, K–8* [Washington, D.C.: National Education Association, 1986].)

Economics and the International Connection
(All Levels)

To provide a more in-depth study of trade and economics around the world, the teacher discusses the role of symbols and trademarks of companies and corporations, and students begin to recognize products and parent companies. Given magazines and newspapers, students create a collage of symbols, trademarks, and/or logos of businesses that have offices or are selling products in the United States. Once the collage is complete, students determine the location of the parent company and mark it on a world map with a miniature picture of the trademark. Lastly, they connect the same trademarks with the same color yarn.

After the trademarks are mounted on the world map, students use the information learned from the map to determine possible trade routes between nations. Then they categorize the trademarks according to the hemisphere and continents where the businesses are located.

Figure 11.1
Competing City Information
(Data to be presented in sequential stages)

Criteria	City A	City B	City C	City D
General statistics	Population 98,000 (Northeast), industrial section	Population 450,000 (Midwest), state capital, part of a 2.5 million metroplex	Population 3,800, isolated rural town (Northwest)	Population 28,000, suburban area (South)
Transportation available	On major river, major rail lines, near large airport on N-S interstate	Has railroad and interstate routes, international airport	On old E-W highway (not interstate) and railroad, airport service available 30 miles away	On major inter-state and rail-road routes, local municipal airport
Tax base	State income tax, extremely high taxes on individuals and businesses	No state income tax, low rates for individuals and businesses	High state income tax, heavy corporate taxes	Low individual and business tax rates, no state income tax

Labor force	Unionized, low productivity, highly skilled workers, adequate supply	Unskilled or semi-skilled, chiefly unionized, supply large, high unemployment	Heavily unionized with timber background, unskilled to skilled workers, low supply	Unskilled and semi-skilled workers, no unions, adequate work force
Utilities	Expensive electricity, water adequate, low supply of gas	Low rates, abundant supplies of electricity, water	Adequate supplies, high rates	Electricity rates low, adequate supplies of gas and water
School system	Above average scores on standardized tests, meets state standards, older buildings	Quality inconsistent, but generally adequate with average test scores, some new buildings	Quality education with limited facilities	Quality above average, funding for education low, but improving (new state law passed)

SOURCE: *Teach-Practice-Apply: The TPA Instruction Model, K–8*, by Judy Reinhartz and David Van Cleaf (Washington, D.C.: National Education Association, 1986), pp. 84–85.

To learn more about these companies and their products, students role play business leaders in the United States who are interested in studying production and workers firsthand by visiting the companies in the country of origin. To prepare for the visit, students go to the library to research the country, its industrial production, etc., using the chart provided in Figure 11.2.

Your Turn

You are developing a lesson on international business to help students understand what is important for the banker and the lending agency to know. Have students assume the role of an American banker who is being asked to make recommendations about the possibilities of offering international loans. Here are a few questions to consider as students prepare for this role:

1. What do I need to know about the country requesting the loan?
   a. What is the language of the country?
   b. What is its culture—customs, traditions, etc?
   c. What is the economic base of the country?
      (1) Major industries
      (2) Urban vs. rural
2.
3.

Figure 11.2
Business Data for _____
(country)

Population	Exports	Physical Characteristics (climate seasons, etc).	Topography	Economic Base (the economy)	Popular Sports	Money Used	Time Zone

Figure 11.2
(continued)

Type of Clothing Worn	Language Spoken	Points of Interest	Educational System	Political System	Geographic Location • latitude • longitude • continent • hemisphere

Chapter 12

GEOGRAPHY AND COMPUTER-BASED INSTRUCTION

In the last 20 years, computers have played a greater role in our daily lives. They have had an impact on instruction in the elementary and secondary schools as well. They have been used to introduce topics, practice skills, and simulate situations or events. Classroom use acquaints students with the way computers operate, the commercial software that is available, and how to write programs in BASIC and LOGO languages.

Teachers at all levels use a variety of instructional strategies and aids—books, films, pictures, and other supplementary materials. The microcomputer is another aid that teachers can use as a way of breathing life into the study of geography in elementary and secondary classrooms. Computer-based instruction can enrich teaching by providing opportunities to—

a. practice skills using drill exercises
b. tutor students
c. simulate and model concepts that are difficult to reproduce in the classroom
d. gather and analyze information
e. use a word processor.

The most popular use of the computer as a classroom aid is for drill and practice exercises. One reason for its use to review and reinforce concepts is the availability of software. The interactive tutorial software programs, on the other hand, require students to get involved by responding to questions or by providing requested information. Simulations require student involvement to a greater degree. The quality of these software programs, which have been developed and produced in the last few years, has improved significantly. And the enthusiasm for computer-assisted instruction is becoming more widespread as more computers are added to elementary and secondary classrooms.

When using this software, students are placed in situations in which they are forced and/or asked to supply information/ideas to keep the program going. They are asked to make decisions, solve problems, and analyze and process information. For example, students in a fourth grade class become a part of a computerized adventure in which they learn about their state by planning a seven-day vacation. While engaged in the simulation, they collect data that they enter into the microcomputer and later use in determining differences in distances and making comparisons (9). Most importantly, computer software links students with the geographer's most traditional tool—the thematic map.

The discussion that follows focuses on a selective number of microcomputer software programs that have been recommended by elementary and secondary teachers. In addition, these programs were selected because they develop geographic skills and concepts, introduce geographic models, and help to develop logical reasoning skills as well as general problem-solving skills. The programs are designed to create a thinking environment in which students develop a critical awareness about their environment as it relates to the curriculum area skills being developed. Most of the software programs that are included are simulations or situational in nature.

The computer as a machine accepts information, works with this information to solve problems, allows individual students or small groups of students to make choices to solve these problems, and provides vicarious experiences—for example, of the Oregon Trail. Many of the programs provide a dimension that makes places, people, cultures, and interactions come alive and become more meaningful to learners as they study social studies, mathematics, and the language arts.

The review of each software program includes (1) the name of the supplier, (2) a description of the program content, and (3) the curriculum area emphasized. The reviews are grouped according to elementary and secondary levels. Readers may want to contact the companies for catalogs and information about other programs.

SOFTWARE PROGRAMS FOR ELEMENTARY
AND MIDDLE SCHOOLS

STICKYBEAR TOWN BUILDER, for *grades 1–3* (from the Society for Visual Education, Inc. [SVE], Department VR, 1345 Diversey Parkway, Chicago, IL 60614-1299), allows young students to construct towns from the ground up. In the process they are introduced to the compass and directions, map reading, positioning and spatial relationships, and vocabulary. After completing and storing up to 20 towns, students, using a compass and directions, can elect to drive their purple car through any of the towns to locate mystery keys. The outcome is an adventure in map skills, location, and basic computer manipulations.

RIVERS AND ANCIENT CULTURES, for *grades 2–8*, in the Teach Yourself series by Computer Software, Inc. (from the Thompson Book and Supply Company, P.O. Box 11600, Oklahoma City, OK 73136), is a relatively inexpensive tutorial on the evolution of Egyptian and Mesopotamian civilizations. It stresses the geographical themes of place, location, and human/environment interactions. The program helps students understand the central roles played by the Nile and the Tigris and Euphrates rivers in the development of these original Bronze Age civilizations. The animated color graphics are even done according to the style and iconography of the ancient Egyptians and Sumerians. Alternate text presentations and review questions and tests are included on each disk.

The ADVENTURES AROUND THE WORLD SERIES, for *grades 3 and up*, by Polarware (also from Thompson), offers adventure games for students to learn about the locations of countries and regions, as well as other information about these areas. Students can experience the adventures in North and South America, Europe, Asia, Africa, and across the Pacific. One to six students can play the games to find the villain or they can use a spy-versus-spy strategy. Given the variations, with each replay students' knowledge of and familiarity with the countries and regions increase.

The GEOGRAPHY SKILLS SERIES, for *grades 5–8*, from Social Studies School Service [SSSS], 102000 Jefferson Boulevard, Room C71, P.O. Box 802, Culver City, CA 90232–0802), introduces geographic data and map skills through tutorials and interactive questions. Six double-sided disks take up the topics of Land Environments, Climates of the World, Time Zones, Mapping, Maps and How to Use Them, and The Vocabulary of Geography. The mapping disk, for example, traces the history of cartography from the ancient Near East to the present and stresses the development of scale, legend, projection, etc. It also shows how to compute metric and nonmetric distances and how to read map symbols. The format makes it easy for students to review the material covered, get help, and record answers.

USA GEOGRAPH and WORLD GEOGRAPH, for *grades 5 and up* (also from SSSS), are versatile, easy-to-use visual geographic databases, consisting of map projections linked with numerous and extensive categories of information. Students can call up the data graphically as maps, graphs, and charts, or textually. Comparisons between different states, countries, and regions and other manipulations of data are encouraged. The programs also are easily customized to serve as take-off points for student research projects in various subject areas and/or reinforcement for classroom presentations by students or their teachers.

THE OREGON TRAIL, for *grades 5 and up*, available from the Minnesota Educational Computing Consortium (also from Thompson), is an extremely popular historical-geographical simulation game that relates to other disciplines such as language arts and mathematics. Students reenact a challenging and eventful trip on the famous Oregon Trail in 1848 from Council Bluffs, St. Joseph, or Independence to Oregon City. Along the way, geographic landmarks are noted and explained, estimates of distances traveled and decisions about expenditures are made, and various probabilities are confronted. Helpful handouts, study guides, and a teacher's guide accompany the program. THE OREGON TRAIL also is a very good program to stimulate elementary students' interest in using computers. A similar program is the very inexpensive OHIO RIVER, from the Ohio Sea Grant Education Program (29 West Woodruff Avenue, Room 059, Columbus, OH 43210–1085).

SOFTWARE PROGRAMS FOR SECONDARY SCHOOLS

EUROPEAN NATIONS AND LOCATIONS, for *grades 4 and up*, by Design Ware (from Thompson), offers a thorough encounter with European geography through which students can learn landforms, capitals, and neighboring countries. To these ends, for example, the program allows students to move countries around Europe into their proper locations on a map. Then students also can go beyond the basics to higher levels with information about historical and current events and relate them over time to the geography of Europe. Unanswered or incorrectly answered questions reappear later to help ensure comprehension of the material.

MAPS AND GLOBES, for *grades 6 and up*, by Micro-Ed (from SVE), is a package of programs with a correlated book to reinforce and expand basic map skills. The various exercises serve to reassure students and build their confidence. The book also is a reference work for the queries posed by computer. Topics range from making and reading maps and globes to landforms, climates, and populations to provide a readily reusable review.

KNOW IT ALL GEOGRAPHY SERIES, for *grades 7–12* (from SSSS), utilizes such familiar childhood games as tic-tac-toe, hangman, bingo, and others to introduce students to significant global and American geographical data and concepts. Games, with simple directions, graphics, and explanations of all questions are included on both disks of this program. Each disk also provides an easy-to-use "teacher game writer" to enable teachers to create new games on any number of topics with varying levels of content difficulty.

MECC DATAQUEST: THE WORLD COMMUNITY, for *grades 7–12* (from SSSS), is a data base package for 27 categories of information on 95 countries around the world. Students can phrase their own questions for the program to answer, develop hypotheses to test, compare and contrast, discern patterns, and draw conclusions. The database is a reference and a research tool.

Similarly, MECC DATAQUEST: LATIN AMERICA provides detailed data on 35 countries of the region south of the United States; MECC DATAQUEST: THE MIDDLE EAST AND NORTH AFRICA does the same for 25 countries in this pivotal arena. There also is MECC DATAQUEST: THE FIFTY STATES for United States geography. All four programs include support manuals with sample lesson plans and strategies, handout masters, and references for teachers.

MALTHUS, for *grades 10–12*, by Albion (also from SSSS), is a computer modeling program to introduce students to demography. It uses a simple classical Malthusian framework to study the linkages between exponential population growth, limited food supplies, and nonrenewable natural resource depletion. By manipulating these three independent variables, students can mathematically calculate and project the catastrophe of a demographic doomsday. In the process, they learn about population control, famine, and resource management, among other topics of current and future interest. The package includes a backup disk, a teacher's guide, and reproducible handouts.

Computer technology can offer an alternative approach to teaching geography because more and more information is handled electronically. Computer-based instruction can enrich geography and other curriculum areas when it is linked to the specific concepts and skills being taught.

PART III. CONCLUSION

Chapter 13

GEOGRAPHIC EDUCATION: LOOKING TO THE FUTURE

This monograph has suggested ways to integrate geography into the school curriculum. All the examples provided deal with some aspect of "place and its dimensions," which are at the heart of geographic education.

The text began with a discussion of the issue of geographic illiteracy, underscoring the need for "information [and knowledge] on geographic education and a concomitant increase in geographic alliances" (17, p. xxvii). Whether it is the lack of knowledge regarding neighbors to the south of the United States (25 percent of students in Dallas could not identify them!) or the inability of students to shade in the United States on a world map (45 percent), teachers and/or students are not the ones to blame. This dilemma has escalated because geography is not an integral part of the current K–12 school curriculum.

As educators, our thinking needs to change about the role and importance of geographic education as it relates to the total general education of students. Knowledge of geography is critical to "seeing the pictures beyond the pictures" to broaden our perspective of the world, to make connections between cause and effect on the earth, and to view events in their proper continuum rather than in isolation (10). Geography can be the gateway to other subjects, cultures, societies, mores, and values, and generally to the world community. Because it is issue-laden, geography builds bridges between disciplines. We certainly are not alone in recommending that geography be a central part of the school curriculum. Patrick (39) reports that in the History-Social Studies Framework for California Public Schools, it is one of the two essential integrated disciplines.

It has not been our intention to encourage elementary and secondary teachers to become geographers, but to assist them in taking advantage of the "geographic descriptions and explanations of events" that are ever present in specific subject areas (17, p. xxv). The integration of geography into both elementary and secondary curricula ensures that students at the end of their schooling can look out a window and make some sense of what they see (18).

It is ludicrous if environmentalists who deal with acid rain are unaware of the wind patterns that exist around the world. Likewise, how can manufacturers remain unaware of world markets and resources? And, how can physicians who are working to eradicate a disease develop a cure without understanding the place where the disease is thriving (18)? Employing a geographic perspective encourages the use of specific measurement tools, qualitative methods, and remote sensing simulation models (2).

Without geographic knowledge that goes beyond a specific subject area, Americans will not "see the tapestry of connections" that forms the mortar that holds the peoples, cultures, and societies together on planet earth. As a nation, our perspective is too narrow; while we may have information, we lack the knowledge we need (10). With such a narrow perspective—assuming our culture is the only one—we see the world as disconnected fragments. "Our earth is showing the wear and tear of years of growth," but the resulting problems provide opportunities (10). To solve the problems, future generations of students need to be connected with their world, and they must have an understanding of geography—location, place, and human environmental interaction—for through it the unity of complex diversity emerges. From a change in perspective comes the beginning of change, and with changes come opportunities that open new vistas to world connections and a brighter future.

It is apparent that geography also offers valuable skills. It is concerned with providing explanations and analyses about places, patterns, spatial networks, and regional comparisons and contrasts. By investigating a place students gather evidence, formulate explanations, trace linkages, examine the process of change, and imagine what it is like to be there. They also increase narrative, verbal, quantitative, and graphic skills. The communication, critical thinking, and decision-making skills gained from the study of geography are readily applicable to other disciplines and situations in education and/or the world of work.

Understanding and appreciation go far beyond knowing facts. Geographic knowledge is purposeful and connected to other subjects in the curriculum. Global resources and their uses, for example, are not necessarily the domain of any single subject or grade level. Through the variety of examples we have presented, teachers at all grade levels have a way of adding a geographic dimension to their subject areas. In all these examples, students are involved in the learning process as they travel abroad on business or for environmental reasons, interact with their peers to solve problems, and analyze cause-and-effect relationships. All the domains of learning (cognitive, affective, and psychomotor) are stressed. Students do geography by having numerous opportunities to experience the many events in society that "occur within a geographic context." Geography is no longer portrayed as a "quiet" subject in the curriculum. Geographic scrutiny is essential to promoting sound decisions about land usage, disposal of chemical waste, global warming, nuclear arms buildup, nuclear power, discrimination, and inequality. Geographic scrutiny may be the most important skill learned through all these hypothetical encounters. Knowing the where and the why of events, which are applicable to all disciplines, is crucial to improving the quality of life on this planet.

The following quotation from Gilbert Grosvenor, who has been instrumental in implementing geographic education programs in schools throughout the United States, aptly summarizes our efforts:

> Geography taught with these fresh ideas and exciting materials can help give students a broad understanding of the world and the cultural, political, economic, and environmental challenges they'll be asked to meet as adults. (22, p. 32)

BIBLIOGRAPHY

1. Arnheim, R. "The Perception of Maps." *American Cartographer* 3 (1976): 5-6.
2. Austin C. M. "Geography and Interdisciplinary, Future-Oriented Education," 1980. ERIC Document Reproduction Service, ED 199 167.
3. Ausubel, D. *Educational Psychology: A Cognitive View*. New York: Holt, Rinehart and Winston, 1968.
4. Backler, Alan. "Teaching Geography in American History," 1988. ERIC Document Reproduction Service, ED 299 222.
5. Balchin, W. C. V., and Coleman, A. M. "Graphicacy Should Be the Fourth Ace in the Pack." *Times Education Supplement* (London), November 5, 1965.
6. Barron, R. F. "The Use of Vocabulary as an Advance Organizer." In *Research in Reading in the Content Areas: First Year Report*, edited by H. L. Herber and P. L. Sanders. Syracuse, N.Y.: Syracuse University Reading and Language Arts Center, 1969.
7. Bruner, J. *The Process of Education*. Cambridge, Mass.: Harvard University Press, 1960.
8. *Census Education Project: 1988*. Washington, D.C.: Department of Commerce, Bureau of the Census, 1988. #DX–3300F.
9. Cirullo, W. D. "Integrating the Computer in Fourth Grade." *Social Education* 51, no. 2 (1987): 139–40.
10. *Connections*. Washington, D.C.: National Geographic Society, 1989. Videotape.
11. Coones, P., and Stoddard, C. V. "A Hundred Years of Geography at Oxford and Cambridge." *Geographical Journal* 155 (March 1989): 13–32.
12. Daugherty, R. *Geography in the National Curriculum*. London: Geographical Association, 1989. ISBN 0 48512 148.
13. Davenport, D. P. "Caravans and Classrooms: The Novel as a Teaching Aid." *Journal of Geography* 80, no. 7 (December 1981): 259–63.
14. *Five Themes of Geography*. Booklet. Washington, D.C.: National Geographic Society, 1988.

15. Forsyth, A. S. Jr. "How We Learn Place Location: Bringing Theory and Practice Together." *Social Education* (November/December 1986): 500–503.
16. Fuller, M. J., and others. "Using State and Local Studies to Teach Geographical Concepts." *Journal of Geography* 81 no. 6 (November-December 1982): 242–45.
17. Gaile, G. L., and Willmont, C. J. *Geography in America.* Columbus, Ohio: Merrill Publishing Co. 1989.
18. *Geography: Making Sense of Where We Are.* Washington, D.C.: National Geographic Society, 1988.
19. Golden, S. E., and Thorndyke, P. W. *Simulating Navigation for Spatial Knowledge Acquisition.* Report No. N–1675–ARMY. Santa Monica, Calif.: Rand Corp. 1981.
20. Goodlad, J. I. "The Learner at World's Center." *Social Education* (October 1986): 424, 436.
21. Grosvenor, G. M. "Geographic Education and Global Understanding." *NASSP Curriculum Report* (September 1986): 2.
22. _____. "The Case for Geography Education." *Educational Leadership* 47, no. 3 (November 1989): 29–32.
23. _____. "Integration of Geography Instruction Urged for Every Subject." *Education USA* 32 (February 1990): 24.
24. *Guidelines for Geographic Education.* Prepared by Joint Committee on Geographic Education. Washington, D.C.: Association of American Geographers, 1984.
25. Holt-Jensen, A. *Geography: History and Concepts—A Student's Guide.* 2d ed. Trans. by Brian Fullerton, Totowa, N.J.: Barnes and Noble Books, 1988.
26. Irwin, J. W., and Baker I. *Promoting Active Reading Comprehension Strategies.* Englewood Cliffs, N.J.: Prentice-Hall, 1989.
27. Kirkwood, T. "Florida Partnership Trains Teachers to Think Globally." *ASCD Curriculum Update.* Washington, D.C.: Association for Supervision and Curriculum Development, January 1989, p. 6.
28. Kirman, J. M. and others. "Integrating Geography with Other School Subjects: A View from an Education Faculty Member. *Journal of Geography* 87, no. 3 (1987): 104–6.
29. Kracht, J. B. "Worth Ten Men on a Rope: A Lesson Plan on Sea Chanties." 1982. ERIC Document Reproduction Service, ED 227 027.

30. Lemlech, J. K. *Curriculum and Instructional Methods for the Elementary School.* New York: Macmillan Publishing Co. 1984.
31. *Mailbox.* "Spanish Fiesta." *Idea Magazine for Teachers.* (December 1988): 21.
32. McNergney, R., and Haberman, M. "To Improve Kids' Writing, Make the Topics Real." *NEA Today* 8, no. 7 (1990): 28.
33. Midgely, S. "British Children Fail to Make the Grade in Global Exam League." *Independent* (London), December 30, 1988, pp. 3, 18–19.
34. _____. "Teachers Oppose Learning by Rote." *Independent* (London), March 29, 1989, p. 3.
35. Muir, S. P., and Cheek, H. N. "A Developmental Mapping Program Integrating Geography and Mathematics," 1983. ERIC Document Reproduction Service, ED 238 796.
36. Natoli, S. J.., and Gritzer, C. F. "Modern Geography." In *Strengthening Geography in the Social Studies.* Bulletin No. 81. Washington, D.C.: National Council for the Social Studies, 1988.
37. O'Neil, J. "Global Education: Controversy Remains, But Support Growing." *ASCD Curriculum Update.* Washington, D.C.: ASCD, January 1989.
38. Parker, E. T., and Conzen, M. P. "Using Maps as Evidence: Lessons in American Social and Economic History," 1975. ERIC Document Reproduction Service, ED 125 395.
39. Patrick, J. "Teaching and Learning Content in the Social Studies: The ERIC/Chess Perspective on Trends and Issues," 1988. ERIC Document Reproduction Service, ED 293 782.
40. Peden, W., ed. *Thomas Jefferson, Notes on the State of Virginia.* Chapel Hill: University of North Carolina Press, 1955, p. 5.
41. Reinhartz, D. "Teaching History with Maps." In *The Visual Display of Quantitative Information,* edited by E. R. Tufte. Cheshire, Conn.: Graphic Press, 1983.
42. Reinhartz, D. "Teaching History with Maps: A Graphic Dimension." In *Walter Prescott Webb and The Teaching of History,* edited by D. Reinhartz and S. E. Maizlish. College Station: Texas A&M University Press, 1985, p. 79.
43. Reinhartz, J., and Reinhartz, D. *Teach-Practice-Apply: The TPA Instruction Model, 7–12.* Washington, D.C.: National Education Association, 1988.

44. Reinhartz, J., and Van Cleaf, D. *Teach-Practice-Apply: The TPA Instruction Model, K–8.* Washington, D.C.: National Education Association, 1986.

45. Rhind, D. "Bad Geography." *Independent* (London), December 30, 1989, p. 19.

46. Robinson, A.; Sale, R.; and Morrison, J. *Elements of Cartography.* 4th ed. New York: John Wiley and Sons, 1978, p. 1.

47. Salter, C. L., and Lloyd, W. J. "Landscape in Literature," 1977. ERIC Document Reproduction Service, ED 157 067.

48. Schwartz, R. H. "Poverty + Hunger = Global Issues." *Journal of Geography* 82, no. 2 (March-April 1983): 76–78.

49. *1990 Science Calendar.* Petaluma, Calif.: Calendars and Books, 1989.

50. *Strength Without Wisdom: A Critique of U.S. Capability.* Washington, D.C.: U.S. Government Printing Office, 1979.

51. Sunal, D. S., and Warask, B. G. "Mapping with Young Children," 1984. ERIC Document Reproduction Service, ED 248 163.

52. *Teaching Geography: A Model for Action.* Washington, D.C.: National Geographic Society, 1988.

53. Texas Education Agency. *State Board of Education Rules for Curriculum: Principles, Standards, and Procedures for Accreditation of School Districts.* Austin, Tex.: State Education Agency, 1985.

54. Wise, J. H. "The Value and Use of Music in Geographic Education," 1979. ERIC Document Reproduction Service, ED 186 337.

55. World Wildlife Fund. *Rain Forest Rap.* Videotape. 6.5 min. World Wildlife Fund, 1250 24th St., N.W., Washington, DC 20036.

GENERAL RESOURCES

ARTICLES

Allenman-Brooks, J.; Clegg, A. A.; and Sebolt, A. P. "Making the Past Come Alive." *Social Studies* 68 (January-February 1977: 6.

Anderson, J. J. "Teaching History by the Audio-Tutorial Method." *History Teacher* 3 (1969): 36–41.

Bailey, P. and Binns, J. A., eds. *A Case for Geography*. London: Geographical Association, 1989.

Balchin, W. C. V., and Coleman, A. M. "Graphicacy Should Be the Fourth Ace in the Pack." *Times Education Supplement* (London), November 5, 1965.

DeVito, A., and Fowler, J. O. "Geography in the Elementary School Isn't Dead, It's Fading." *School Science and Mathematics* 70, no. 6 (June 1970): 511–14.

Eddy, R., and others. "River Trek. Teacher Guide and Activity Book," 1987. OEAGLS Investigation No. 26. ERIC Document Reproduction Service, ED 285 740.

Kronowitz, E. "From Customs to Classroom." *Social Studies Review* 24, no. 3 (1985): 68–73.

Martin, E. C., and Sandler, M. W. "Rejuvenating the Teaching of United States History." *Social Education* 7 (1971): 733–37.

Olmstead, C. W. "Knowing and Being Who We Are." *Journal of Geography* 86, no. 1 (January-February 1987): 3–4.

Pannivitt, B., ed. "Locating Geography on the Curriculum Map," 1986. ERIC Document Reproduction Service, ED 281 786.

Parker, W. "How to Help Students Learn History and Geography." *Educational Leadership* 47, no. 3 (November 1989): 39–43.

Parry, J. H. "Old Maps Are Slippery Witnesses." *Harvard Magazine* 32 (April 1976).

"Population, Plenty and Poverty." *National Geographic*, December 1988.

Priestland, A. "Willesdon High School: Local Studies Project—Summer Term 1985." *Bulletin of Environmental Education*, No. 179 (April 1986): 12–14.

Reinhartz, D. "The Remapping of Civilization: An Artifactual Approach to Teaching World History." *Proceedings of the Sixth International Conference on Improving University Teaching*. Lausanne, Switzerland (College Park, University of Maryland), July 1980, pp. 911–12.

Roberts, M.: "Using Videocassettes." *Teaching Geography* 12, no. 3 (1987): 114–17.

Rushdoony, H. A. "Integrating Reading and English—Language Arts in the Geography Curriculum," 1982. ERIC Document Reproduction Service, ED 232 959.

Sack, D. "The Popularity of Grade–School Geography: A Texas Case Study." Unpublished manuscript, University of Utah, 1987.

Souze, A. R. "Software for Geographers: Programs and Vendors." *Journal of Geography* 84, no. 2 (March-April 1985): 81–82.

Walford, R. "Geography Games and Simulations: Learning Through Experience." *Journal of Geography in Higher Education* 5, no. 2 (October 1981): 113–19.

Walsh, S. J. "Geographic Information Systems: An Instructional Tool for Earth Science Educators." *Journal of Geography* 87, no. 1 (January-February 1988): 17–25.

Watson, W. J. *Mental Images and Geographical Reality in the Settlement of North America*. Nottingham, U.K.: University of Nottingham, Cust Foundation Lecture, 1967.

Whitmore, P. M. "Mapping a Course. *Science and Children* 25, no. 4 (January 1988): 15–17.

Wolf, A. "100 Jahre Putzger—100 Jahre Geschichtsbild in Deutschland (1877–1977)" (100 Years of Putzger—100 Years of Historical Maps in Germany [1877–1977]), *Geschichte in Wissenschaft und Unterricht* 29 (1978): 702–18.

Zuckerman, D. W., and Horn, R. E. "The Guide to Simulations/Games for Education and Training," June 1973. ERIC Document Reproduction Service, ED 072 667.

BOOKS

Adventures in Your National Parks (3–8). National Geographic Society. $9.50. No. 00707.

Bargrow, L., and Skelton, R. A. *History of Cartography*. Cambridge, Mass.: Harvard University Press, 1964.

Boardman, D. *Graphicacy and Geography Teaching*. London: Croom Helm, 1983.

Brown, L. A. *The Story of Maps*. New York: Dover Publications, 1977.

Geo-whiz, Why on Earth (3–8). National Geographic Society. $9.50. No. 00662.

Harley, B. W., and Woodward, D. *History of Cartography*. Vol. 1. Chicago: University of Chicago Press, 1987.

Living on Earth (High School). (1988). National Geographic Society. $31.95. No. 00736.

Malthus, T. R. *Essay on the Principle of Population*. New York: W. W. Norton and Co., 1976.

Martin, J. C., and Martin, R. S. *Maps of Texas and the Southwest, 1513–1900*. Albuquerque: University of New Mexico Press, 1984.

Montesquieu, B. C. *Spirit of Laws*. New York: Free Press, 1969.

Peden, W., ed. *Thomas Jefferson, Notes on the State of Virginia*. Chapel Hill: University of North Carolina Press, 1955, p. 5.

Schwartz, S., and Ehrenberg, R. E. *The Mapping of America*. New York: Harry N. Abrams, 1980.

Southworth, M., and Southworth, S. *Maps: A Visual Survey and Design Guide*. Boston: Little, Brown and Co., 1982.

Turner, F. J. *The Frontier in American History*. Tucson: University of Arizona Press, 1985.

Webb, W. P. *The Great Frontier*. Austin, Tex.: University of Texas Press, 1964.

Webb, W. P. *The Great Plains*. New York: Grosset and Dunlap, 1931.

Wilford, J. N. *The Mapmakers*. New York: Alfred A. Knopf, 1981.

FILM/VIDEOS

1. *Geography: A Voyage of Discovery.* (6–12). National Geographic Society. $15.00. No. 50458.

2. *Physical Geography of North America* (4–9). National Geographic Society. Series of six videos (VHS). $431.75. No. 51357.

3. *Pollution: World at Risk* (Senior High). National Geographic Society. $99.95. No. 51355.

FILMSTRIPS

Our World (K–4), Series (1989).
Explores relationships common to human societies around the world—families, schools, neighborhoods, communities, countries and earth. National Geographic Society. Parts I, II, III, $67.00 each.

Portraits of the Continents (5–9), Series (1988).
Explores the major geographic features of the continents. National Geographic Society. Parts I and II, $67 each; Part III, $90.

GAMES

1. Global Pursuit (6–12) (1987).
   National Geographic Society. $19.95. No. 80500.

LOCATION OF RESOURCES

The Geographical Journal
of the Royal Geographical Society
London, England

Historic Urban Plans
Box 276
Ithaca, NY 14850

Imago Mundi
Journal of the International Society
for the History of Cartography
Lympne Castle, Kent, England

Mapline
Hermon Dunlap Smith
Center for the History of Cartography
The Newberry Library
60 West Walton Street
Chicago, IL 60610

The Map Collector
Tring: Map Collector Publications, Ltd.
P.O. Box 53
Tring, Herts. England
11P 23 5 BH

National Geographic Society
For orders, inquiries, and catalogs
1-800-368-2728. In Maryland,
1-301-821-1330 or write
National Geographic Society
Educational Services
Washington, DC 20036

Terrae Incognitae
Journal of the Society for
the History of Discoveries
Barbara McCorkle, Secretary-Treasurer
45 Mill Rock Road
Hamden, CT 06511

"U.S. Population Data Sheet"
"World Population Data Sheet"
(both published annually)
Population Reference Bureau, Inc.
777 14th Street, N.W., Suite 800
Washington, DC 20005
(202) 639-8040

MAPS

Historical Atlas of the United States (9–12) (1988)
National Geographic Society
$59.95, No. 00747; $74.95, No. 00748.

Martin, R. S., and Martin, J. C. *Contours of Discovery: Printed Maps Delineating the Texas and Southwestern Chapters in the Cartographic History of North America.* Austin: Texas State Historical Association, 1981–82 (22 maps).

SLIDES

Kish, G. *The Discovery and Settlement of North America, 1500–1865. A Cartographic Perspective.* New York: Harper and Row, Publishers, 1978. 203 slides and cassette tape.

TELECOMMUNICATIONS

Kids Network
Telecommunications-based science curriculum for grades 4–6.
National Geographic Society

The Weather Machine (7–12)
Includes software, a filmstrip, student booklets, lesson plans, and activity sheets. Available for 128K Apple IIe, IIc, and IIGS Computers.
National Geographic Society

PC Globe
A computerized world atlas
Comwell Systems, Inc.
2100 South Rural Road, Suite 2
Tempe, AZ 85282
$69.95 and $4.00 shipping and handling

WORKBOOKS

Teaching Geography: A Model for Action
Mark Sanders, Teaching Geography Project
National Geographic Society